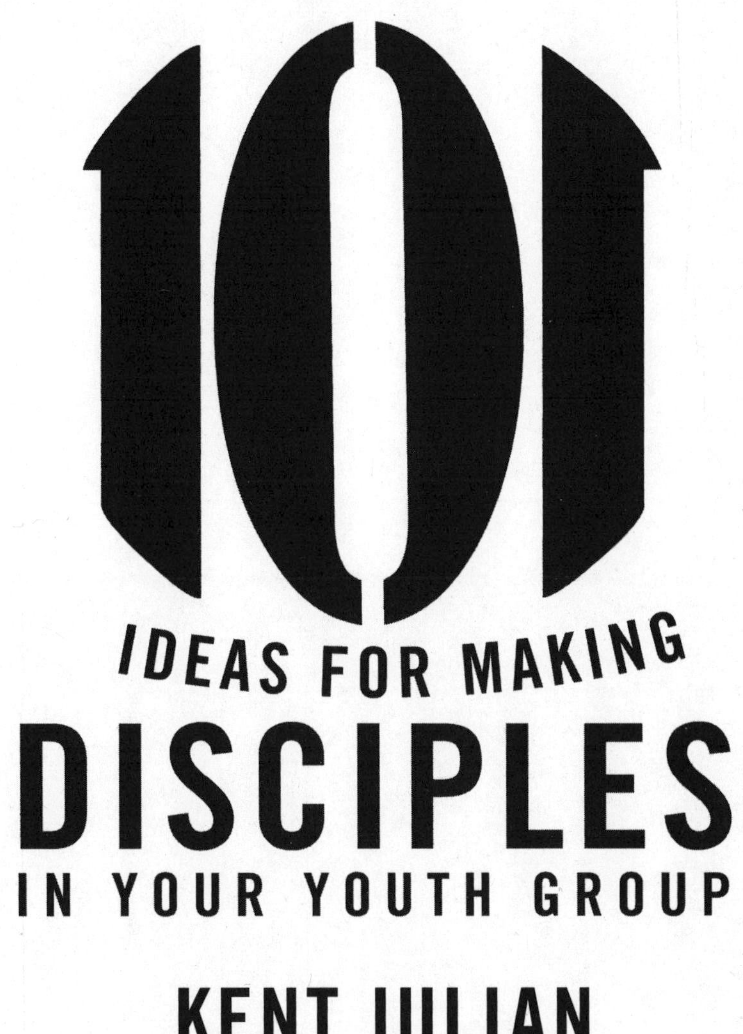

101 IDEAS FOR MAKING DISCIPLES IN YOUR YOUTH GROUP

KENT JULIAN

101
IDEAS FOR MAKING
DISCIPLES
IN YOUR YOUTH GROUP
KENT JULIAN

ZONDERVAN®

ZONDERVAN.com/
AUTHORTRACKER
follow your favorite authors

youth
specialties

101 Ideas for Making Disciples in Your Youth Group

Youth Specialties resources, 300 S. Pierce St., El Cajon, CA 92020 are published by Zondervan, 5300 Patterson Ave. SE, Grand Rapids, MI 49530.

ISBN 978-0-310-27495-7

Cover design by Toolbox Studios
Interior design by David Conn

Printed in the United States of America

08 09 10 11 12 • 20 19 18 17 16 15 14 13 12 11 10 9 8 7 6 5 4 3 2 1

TO SONLIFE MINISTRIES

This book is dedicated to all the incredible people I have met over the years through my connection with **Sonlife Ministries**. Each of you impacted me. Specifically, during my first 10 years with Sonlife, people such as Dann Spader, Don Roscoe, Jack Perrine, and Ed Short *shaped* my understanding of ministry. During the past 10 years, people such as Bill Clem, Rob Yonan, Luke Hendrix, Mike Harder, Erik Liechty, John Zivonjinovic, Dave Livermore, and Steve Argue *strengthened* my philosophy of ministry. In the next 10 years, I sense that the two new men at the helm of Sonlife, Chris Folmsbee and Mike Novelli, will *stretch* my thinking of ministry. I look forward to the adventure!

CONTENTS

PART 4

INTRODUCTION
POLAROID CAMERAS AND DISCIPLE MAKING

*Spiritual formation in a Christian tradition answers a specific human question: "What kind of person am I going to be?" It is the **PROCESS** of establishing the character of Christ in a person. That's all it is.*

- Dallas Willard -

Christianity Today, July 2005

I love flipping through my vintage stacks of youth ministry photos. Some pictures jog memories of all the God stuff that's happened over the years:

- After Alex's enormously difficult sophomore year, seeing him follow Jesus was not in the realm of reality. No way, not in my wildest dreams...but it happened.
- And what about Nancy? Once afraid of her shadow, now she carries herself with such grace and confidence.
- And these are just two pictures from this pack. Other snapshots are of students who introduced peers to Jesus, parents who restored relationships with kids, and individuals who moved from denying Christ to deeply loving him. I couldn't make this stuff up or force it to happen; I was simply lucky enough to be in the right place at the right time to click the camera.

There's another pile I like to thumb through—those over-the-top photos that put a wide, toothy grin on this ugly mug. I'm sure you have a similar stack—bare-chested, swimsuit-wearing, senior guys running around at snow camp. Middle school boys weighing no more than 85 pounds flying down the waterslide we nicknamed "The Wedge-ie." Spam-eating (er, upchucking) contests. Water-balloon launchers skyrocketing fruitcakes during a Christmas bash. Ah, what memories!

Yet of all the stacks cluttering my office, the winner for most memorable moments comes from my old school scavenger hunt heap. You know, those Polaroid photos taken with that classic 1970s camera? Unlike today's digital photos, these instant snapshots required a bit more time to process and usually meant at least one team member had to have the handshaking aptitude of a presidential candidate or the lung capacity of an Olympic swimmer. I can still envision Andy viciously shaking his most creative picture, or Josh turning various shades of lavender in a vain attempt to blow his snapshot into focus faster. These two guys had to make sure they captured the perfect shot before moving to the next idiotic—and in some states, illegal—stunts on the list: Manning a McDonald's register—200 points; handstands in an elevator—500 points; standing in a fountain—750 points; locked behind prison bars—1,000 points; TPing the senior pastor's house—1,500 points; forking the lawn of the grumpy deacon who wears the same lime-green leisure suit and sits in the third row every Sunday morning—50,000 points.

FROM BLURRY TO...BLURRIER

Vintage scavenger-hunt photos bring back memories—good memories. Yet they also capture the essence of a vision quest with which most youth workers are all too familiar.

In their commitment to make disciples of Jesus Christ among students, many youth workers race from seminar to seminar and conference to conference, frantically searching for the right ministry model. If they happen to stumble across one that resonates with them, they snap a plethora of photos and then confidently venture back to the real world trenches believing their new photos hold the secrets to success. But in their attempts to process these snapshots, something happens: The pictures are underdeveloped. No matter what they try, no matter how vigorously they shake or blow on the snapshots, the fuzziness doesn't dissipate. The picture merely transforms from blurry...to blurrier. They discover few elements from this new strategy fit their contexts, and within a matter of months, they're back to square one.

Disheartened, these youth workers chalk up their disappointment to, "It just wasn't the right workshop for me," and promise themselves they'll never get fooled again. But eventually new four-color glossy brochures float across their desks. A new conference promises a cutting-edge approach guaranteed to deliver the goods. Their pulses quicken! Their hearts skip a beat. Calculating next year's budget, they figure a way to squeeze it in. Yes, God answers prayer. "This time," they proclaim, "I'll find real success!"

NO MORE SCAVENGER HUNTS...

Ever met a youth worker like that? Let's get a bit more personal: *Ever been a youth worker like that?* (My hand is up.)

Youth ministry training is tremendous. Every year I go to at least one conference, and I'm a bookaholic, like most other youth workers. So I'm in no way slamming conferences, training, books, or resources. To the contrary, I'm exceedingly grateful for these tools.

But I admit there was a time, an extensive period of time, when I hopped from conference to conference and resource to resource in search of *the* magic plan. It's as if I were on a scavenger hunt, looking for the perfect approach for making disciples among students—an approach that would fit any situation or context. In my mind, if I found it, I could take it back to my church, implement it step by step, and finally achieve true success in ministry. But I discovered that the "right approach" to disciple making isn't a cut-and-paste exercise. Just because something works for others doesn't necessarily mean it'll work for me. There's no one-size-fits-all plan.

So what's a youth worker to do?

...BUT DON'T THROW OUT YOUR POLAROID CAMERA

Although developing a disciple-making environment in youth ministry is tricky, it can be done. While we need to stop our scavenger hunt for the perfect, one-size-fits-all approach, we don't need to throw out our Polaroid cameras, either. In fact, cultivating an authentic disciple-making ministry, one in which students are transformed into genuine followers of Christ, is similar to the process by which a Polaroid photo develops.

First, youth workers must know where to find an accurate picture of a disciple-making environment. (They're out there, believe it or not. And notice the accurate picture is an "environment," not an "approach" or "plan"—more on this in a moment.) Then, once a youth worker locks on to that picture, everything from lessons to activities and trips and relationships must congeal together…over time…to bring the snapshot into contextual focus. Again, pretty similar to the way a Polaroid photo is processed.

WHAT THIS BOOK IS NOT

Before diving into what exactly this book is, it's important to be clear about what this book is not:

This book is NOT an endorsement for a specific plan. It's my hope that this book doesn't come across as being the latest, end-all mantra regarding a new youth ministry philosophy, purpose, mission, vision, or whatever other term might be used to communicate successful ministry approaches. While this book's focus is on cultivating an environment for making disciples within a youth ministry context, you won't find in these pages a specific, new-fangled, innovative, one-size-fits-all plan. From the start, my desire is to write about the environmental issues behind students transforming into disciples of Jesus, not the specifics of a particular plan. Admittedly, trying to fully articulate this desire up front is difficult, but just saying it from the get-go should prepare you for what's ahead and perhaps pique your interest to read further. And as you read, I believe the environmental intent of this book will develop, much like a Polaroid photo coming into focus.

This book is NOT an endorsement of a specific structure. There's no attempt to convince you that certain programs are vital or that other programs must be disbanded. You'll find no coercive words about small groups, house groups, student-led groups, grade-level groups, specific gender groups, large-event outreaches, Sunday school, 5th Quarters, youth choirs, Bible quizzing, camping, mission trips, service projects, or midweek programming. While structures are mentioned, all discussion is for illustrative purposes, not endorsement. In other words, the ideas discussed in the following pages should help regardless of your ministry structure.

WHAT THIS BOOK IS

So what *is* this book about?

This is a missional book. Personally, no word inspires loftier living for me than *missional*. The idea of missional living revolves around "the Mission of God (often called *missio Dei*) in this world; it is holistic—including both evangelism and social action; it does not divide evangelism from social action. It's central concern is to incarnate the gospel in a community; it is concerned with reaching out ('How can we help?') along with attracting folks 'to church.'"[1] In my mind, missional living is intimately tied to cultivating an environment within my life and ministry for making disciples. I can't hold on to one without grasping the other, so I can't write a book about making disciples without talking about missional living.

This is a contextual book. As already indicated, this book fully embraces the belief that there is no end-all, overarching, supra-contextual, one-size-fits-all approach to making disciples. While I do believe certain environmental elements should be present in any disciple-making ministry, the strategies for nurturing these elements will vary according to context. Therefore, helping you contextualize your approach to fit your specific settings and surroundings is at the heart of this book. This doesn't mean the book goes into detail about how to contextualize ministry; it doesn't. It simply means the spirit behind what's written is to help you think more deeply about the transformation of students, so you can determine whether your approach helps or hinders their development as followers of Christ in your own context.

This is an environmental book. At my core, I'm an environmentalist. My vocabulary is drenched with environmental imagery, and if you rub shoulders with me long enough, you'll get environmentally soaked. But before Greenpeace or Sierra Club members bow down and call me blessed, the environmentalism I promote is not exactly the kind they highlight. Don't get me wrong; I respect the ecosystem. But I'm more passionate about another cause. Let's just say I'm zealous about cultivating green space conducive to seeing God transform the lives of students. Call it creating a God-focused ozone that others can literally feel when they're in it.

Now here's the kicker. As a youth worker, I don't see my role in the disciple-making process as that of a "producer," but rather as an "environmental officer." In other words, my role is to cultivate environments in which disciples can be developed, while simultaneously downplaying my role for producing transformation. Jesus might choose to use me in the change process according to his purposes, but *he* is the one who brings about change. While this might sound

> *He will therefore have to use what knowledge he can achieve, not to shape the results as the craftsman shapes his handiwork, but rather to cultivate a growth by providing the appropriate environment, in the manner in which the gardener does this for his plants.*
>
> **—Friedrich August von Hayek**

radical, a believer's job is not and has never been to create life change. That's God's job, and God's job only. What this means is that the more we try to take on the responsibility of changing others, the less effective we become.

Don't mishear what's being said—everything we do as youth workers should be about life change...up to the point of trying to make it happen. Why? Because no matter how hard we try, we *cannot* manufacture it. God transforms, pure and simple, and God does so according to his timetable and purposes. As God's followers, our only job, then, is to cultivate environments that allow God to do his thing when and where he wants. This book, therefore, focuses on the environmental role youth workers play in making disciples while they trust God to focus on his life-changing, transformational role.

This is a process book. Not "process" as in "Take Steps A, B, and C so you can get to Destination D." That's an assembly-line approach, and assembly lines don't work too well in regard to personal transformation. However, as stated previously, this book focuses on a process similar to a Polaroid photo being developed. If youth workers focus on the right vision and capture that image, over time the elements of that picture should congeal together, and a solid, disciple-making photo should come into focus.

By the way...throughout the book I'll be mixing the Polaroid and environmental metaphors since both are crucial to understanding disciple making. However, since youth workers are some of the smartest people I know, I'm not too worried; you can handle a few mixed metaphors.

This is a holistic book. Instead of leaning exclusively toward practicality or philosophy, this book attempts to balance both. In the first section, a biblical picture of making disciples is discussed; the second section makes this missional call practical by giving 101 ideas for cultivating a transformational environment for disciple making.

MY DESIRE

My desire is to offer you a better vision of making disciples in youth ministry than the one you might currently embrace. It's not a one-size-fits-all strategy or program, but a missional, contextual, environmental, process-oriented, and practical picture. My articulation of this picture won't be perfect, and not all the ideas shared will fit your context. But if this book gets the right kind of conversations stirred up and gives you a few ideas for cultivating an environment for transformation, then it will accomplish its purpose.

So, if you're ready, pull out that Polaroid camera and begin taking some disciple-making snapshots.

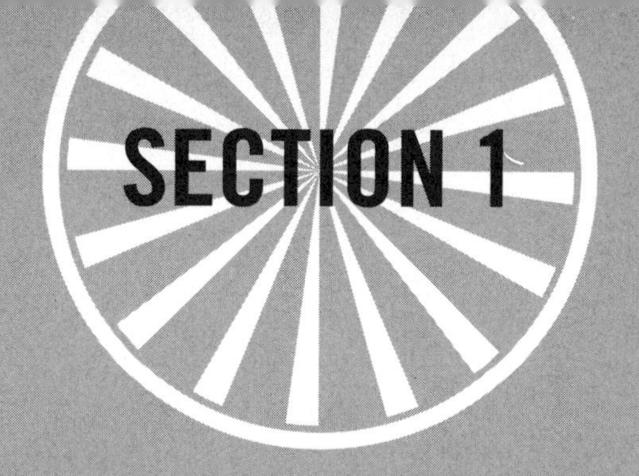

CLICK—BEGIN WITH THE END IN MIND

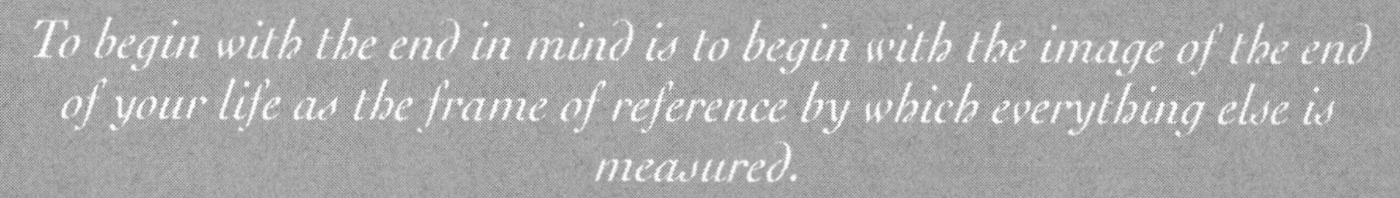

To begin with the end in mind is to begin with the image of the end of your life as the frame of reference by which everything else is measured.

- Stephen Covey -

The Seven Habits of Highly Effective People

"Begin with the end in mind" is based on the principle that all things are created twice. There's a mental or first creation, and a physical or second creation to all things.

- Stephen Covey -

The Seven Habits of Highly Effective People

(God's) intent was that now, through the church, the manifold wisdom of God should be made known to the rulers and authorities in the heavenly realms, according to his eternal purpose that he accomplished in Christ Jesus our Lord.

- The Apostle Paul -

(Ephesians 3:10-11)

IMAGINE

People only see what they are prepared to see.

- Ralph Waldo Emerson -

What follows is a true story that happened in a ministry I was privileged to lead. It's retold from memory and from my vantage point. There are no exaggerations for effect—it's the real deal from an average guy who, in spite of himself, has seen God do some extraordinary things. (Also, the names of students have been changed for privacy.)

GOD STUFF IS GOING TO HAPPEN

It was the Wednesday night before our Mission Mexico trip, and the adult leaders were crammed into my puny living room for a final touch-base meeting. This trip had become tradition (Mark Oestreicher actually started it before I became the youth pastor), and although there were a handful of first-time leaders, most had been part of the expedition before and viewed the whole experience as old-hat. Yet for some reason, this time there was a feeling of anticipation. No one could put a finger on the what, why, or how—we simply knew this trip wasn't going to be routine. So this night felt different from past final meetings. Our expectations were higher. There was a nervous energy. Our prayer was hope-filled and dependent. We wanted to be ready because we sensed God stuff might happen.

A bit of context is probably necessary. This was a middle school mission trip. More specifically, it was for students who'd completed eighth grade and would be entering ninth grade within a matter of weeks. And the trip wasn't open to just anyone. Students had to have been committed to our group, demonstrated a growing relationship with Christ, and articulated a genuine desire to cultivate relationships with peers so God, in his timing and according to his purposes, could use our students to bring others to himself. This next part might sound too stringent for some, but every year there were students who applied who we wouldn't allow to go. Yes, we made students apply and interview. And yes, we were willing to say "no" if we sensed students weren't ready. We believed it was our duty to graciously speak truth into their lives instead of being dishonest with them. Plus, we wanted to keep the expectations and requirements for this team high, so we screened accordingly.

Preparation for the trip was intense—extensive training meetings, service projects, personal devotions, and high accountability. It was so intense, in fact, that students often had to decide between our team and some other significant opportunity.

For instance, during this particular year one student had to choose between being on a traveling baseball team and being part of the Mexico team. Another had to pick between a statewide singing company and our team. Since it was our conviction that this team was as high a calling as any other endeavor, we weren't willing to allow membership to take a back seat to anything. Forcing these kinds of choices was a good thing. We weren't trying to be legalistic, just wanting to raise the bar because the trip was more than an event; it was a catalyst in cultivating students who were committed to being disciples and doing the work of disciple making.

What's more, our team's vision was similar to what David Livermore articulates in his excellent book, *Serving with Eyes Wide Open: Doing Short-Term Missions with Cultural Intelligence*. There was a strong desire to develop a community of students committed to being "world Christians," which we defined as Christians who are unselfish with time, service, money, and prayer. It meant helping students develop a sincere concern for people who don't know Christ and a willingness to go beyond the security of their peer groups into the unknown of building authentic relationships and extending a verbal witness for Christ. It was all about helping students live missionally, no matter where they might be in the world.

GOD STUFF HAPPENED

God stuff did happen that year. I've led many mission trips, but this one was special. I still speak of it from time to time when making presentations, and rarely can I finish without a lump forming in my throat (or worse, blubbering like a baby). Here's what happened.

Our ministry had this mission trip down; not in such a way that we dictated to our partner church how ministry should be done, but in such a way that we were prepared to do whatever the church needed us to do to serve their needs in the following areas:

- Construction—building church structures, building homes; no matter what we did, we partnered with people in the church and followed their lead
- Prayer—prayer walks, prayer meetings, praying for the sick...you name it, we prayed for it; and again, we followed the church's lead
- Evangelism—sports evangelism, door-to-door evangelism, showing the *Jesus* movie, or whatever the church felt was best for the community
- Children's ministry—VBS, neighborhood clubs, sports programs, or again, anything the church felt would best serve its purposes

I was always proud of our groups. Each was trained to be flexible and culturally proficient, and most surpassed expectations, especially for eighth graders.

But mission trips have never made my top-10 list of youth ministry experiences. There are various reasons, but primarily I hate the role I feel forced to play. I'm always the bad guy. The guy who says, "No...nada... sorry, but we can't do that. We're already overcommitted, and there's no way we can do anything else to help." What's worse, I even *look* like a bad guy. I'm a bald-headed, goatee wearing, thick-necked, stocky guy who's called "Stone Cold" by most Mexican kids on our trips. Believe me, I'm a mini, mini, mini version of the wrestler Stone Cold Steve Austin; and while my looks might make me popular with Mexican kids, they just make me look mean when I tell their parents, "No, we can't help."

So this is a part of the leadership gig I'd gladly give up. In fact, each year I've tried different approaches to make the job stink a little less. One year I tried the time-frame concept: "We are here for only five days and don't have time to build anything else." The next year I gave the prescreening explanation: "Sorry, but the church picked which homes we would build before we arrived." No matter what approach I took, the throng of people needing help expanded each year. And with each passing summer, I hated this job more.

DAY 1

This particular summer was the nastiest. I saw more people my first day than I had ever seen before. What's worse, something was broken inside of me. My heart had somehow moved from compassion to contempt. As I looked at the overwhelming need, I actually conjured up the belief that these people weren't doing enough to help themselves. I'm ashamed to admit it, but I was counting the hours until we could load up and head back to camp.

Back at camp, we did the usual thing: Cleaned up, ate dinner, and then gathered together for processing what we believed God was doing in and through us. I wasn't in the state of mind to lead, and I had long ago forgotten about any God stuff happening. So when something out of the ordinary began to happen—I got ticked.

Two students told about how they had met a woman with a small baby. Through a translator, this woman explained that her son needed to see a doctor. Not too bad yet. But then they said, "We promised her if she came to our worksite tomorrow, we would take her and her son to a clinic."

My mind exploded. *What? Who told you to say that? Didn't we train you over and over not to make promises to people? We even explained this was one of the hardest parts of a mission experience—seeing more needs than can be met. How could you have made such a promise? You've set me up. Tomorrow, once again, I'm going to look like the big, bad, bald-headed guy who won't do anything for anyone!*

Before I could speak one word, the point person from the mission organization that was facilitating our trip jumped in and said, "I think we should pray about what God wants to do through us to help this lady." *What!?! Are you kidding? Pray about it? You're the one who taught me to train students not to make promises, and now you're supporting it? Besides, who gave you the reigns of this meeting? I'm leading this trip; you're just facilitating!*

I was officially way beyond being steamed, but what could I do? I had to go along with what was happening. But as the evening came to an end, I reminded students why we couldn't make promises, then I heaped on an extra serving of guilt to make sure everyone knew how miserable this was going to be for me, the bad guy who had to say "no."

Once the meeting broke up, I made a beeline to Seth, the facilitator, and laid into him. "What are you thinking? These are eighth-graders! You're getting their hopes up as if we can do something. We've already committed to an aggressive agenda *before* the trip. You've said yourself that we're the best prepared group you've ever worked with, and that we get more accomplished than almost any other group—including adults. Plus, you're the one who told me to make sure students don't make promises about how we can help. Yet tonight, instead of backing me, you made me look like the bad guy for doing what you taught me to do. What were you thinking?"

Seth calmly replied, "I was thinking perhaps God might want to do something unique with your group. I'm not sure, but I sensed praying was a good risk to take."

"Well, I didn't sense anything! And don't you ever do that to me again!"

With that, I walked away, totally missing out on what God was already doing.

DAY 2

We had no idea where this lady lived or how to contact her. As a matter of fact, when we pressed the two students for information, they pointed to the desert and said, "She lives out there."

"There is nothing out there except sand," I said. "No water. No roads. Nothing!"

But these two students were adamant. "That's where she lives!"

So we came up with a plan that in my mind was sure to fail (and let's be honest, I wanted it to fail). Here's what we decided:

1. If the lady showed up at our worksite during the day, we'd see if we could help. But if she didn't show up on that day, there would be nothing we could do.
2. I made one other concession: Since the two students were convinced this lady needed our help, I allowed them to spend the morning looking for her. I had never done this before, and I wasn't doing it because I cared; I just didn't want anybody tagging me as the guy who didn't do enough. So I allowed these two students, along with two adults, to fill numerous canteens and walk into the desert. They had to walk east in a straight line and had to promise to never lose sight of the community where we were working. They could walk for 60 minutes max before turning around and heading back.

That was the plan. Before these four individuals left, our group prayed. All 40 students and 12 adults prayed that somehow this lady would be found. Secretly, I prayed for the opposite.

At the day's end, the lady hadn't shown up, and our exploration group hadn't found her. Disappointment was painted on everyone's face, and while my face looked sad, there was an extra spring in my step. Well, put yourself in my shoes. I was tired of giving hopeless news to people who desperately needed hope. Coldhearted? Try "emotional survival." I had forgotten all about God stuff and was only trying to make it through the day without crushing anyone else's spirit.

Every van but one had loaded up and left for the day. As I was packing up the last bucket of hammers, my walkie-talkie erupted with excitement. "Kent…Kent…she's here…they're here…they made it!"

"Who's here?" I barked.

"The lady and her baby!"

(Long, long, long pause) "Bring them over to the church."

There was now a different kind of spring in my step. I was ticked again. *Why couldn't we have gotten out of here five minutes earlier?*

I had prepared my bad guy speech before Alex and Holly arrived with the young mother and child. "We simply cannot help. We've used all our resources to build these three homes and to help with the addition to the church. These projects were determined by the church before we arrived, and they are all we can do. I wish we could help, but we simply don't have the resources."

Then I turned to look at the mother and child.

I saw panic in her eyes. She was holding her son, who at six months looked like a skeleton. Soon tears were streaming down my cheeks. The first words I uttered were, "We HAVE to do something for this boy!"

A bit more context here. At that moment I had no idea if this baby's sickness was going to be inexpensive or costly to cure, or if it could even be cured. All I knew was a willingness to do anything and everything to help. Why?

Because Christopher, my firstborn, was six months old at the time and was on this trip.

Since my wife grew up in Peru and speaks fluent Spanish, we really wanted her to be a part of the Mexico team, which meant our infant son came with us on the trip. We had lined up people to take care of Christopher during the day, and he stayed with us at night. It made for a crazy trip, but looking back, having my son with me added to the impact of what I was experiencing.

There was only one difference between the two baby boys: My son had been born in the United States. The boy I was looking at had a mother and father who loved him just as much as Kathy and I loved Christopher; I could see it in her eyes. But she had no options, and I had many. This simple truth put everything into context for me, and that's why we HAD to do something.

Manuel and his mother went to the hospital. It was discovered he had salmonella poisoning. Fifteen dollars of medicine, and he'd be fine. Without it he'd have likely died. Fifteen dollars to save a life!

Afterward, as we drove Manuel and his mother, Claudia, back to their home, we started driving into the desert. Every few minutes, I would interrupt my wife and Claudia's conversation to say, "Kathy, ask her again if we're heading in the right direction." Each time she indicated we were, which was hard to believe since there was *nothing* out there. Finally I said, "Kathy, are you sure you understand what she's saying?" Kathy looked back at me with a smirk and said, "Which one of us speaks Spanish?"

We finally arrived at Claudia's home, and once again my tears began to flow. As I've indicated, I've been on numerous mission trips to various countries, but never had I seen a more desperate situation. This family was living in the 120-degree desert with no water, no facilities...no nothing! Their home consisted of two 4x4 propped up walls made of wooden planks and a bed sheet draped over the top to serve as the roof. Thousands upon thousands of flies hovered around the food, human excrement, and us.

Here's how desperate the situation was: Our construction leader, Rollie, walked back to the van. A minute later I walked over to the van to get water for the family. Rollie is one of the toughest guys I have ever met. Imagine this kind of guy: If he ever accidentally cut off his thumb with a skill saw, he'd look you in the eye and say, "Pick up my thumb, brush off the sawdust, and let's get to the emergency room." There'd be no tears. No shrieks of horror. No feeling sorry for himself. If anything, he'd be ticked for making such a stupid mistake.

And there was Rollie, crying like a baby. It was such an authentically hilarious moment; we both busted out laughing. We laughed, and we cried, and I finally got it: *God stuff was happening!*

That night during our processing gathering, the students who were in the last van shared with the rest of the group what had happened. Everyone sensed the eternal significance of the moment—for Claudia and her family, for our partner church, for the community, and for our group. We had no idea what we were supposed to do, but we agreed we had to do something. What's more, I felt compelled to confess my lack of faith and inept leadership.

I confessed that I believed God had been preparing me for this trip, but it had taken a 2x4 to the side of my skull to see what God was doing.

For the next few hours we prayed, shared ideas, and prayed some more. Finally, late into the night, we developed the following faith-based plan:

We believed God wanted us to build a house for this family. We believed he wanted the house to be near the church and built with the help of the people in the church and Claudia's husband, who we had yet to meet. To do this, several obstacles had to be overcome:

1. We had no property on which to build the house. Seth, the trip facilitator, indicated that a plot of land in this community would cost about $1,200, but the biggest hurdle would be getting through the governmental red tape fast enough. According to Seth, it could take months to negotiate buying property, and we had only three days.
2. We needed another $1,000 for building supplies. We had no money left. Whatever money we were going to use had to be raised through the offering of 40 eighth-graders and a handful of adults. We had always taken an offering during past trips and the highest amount ever received was $800. That wouldn't even be enough for building materials, not to mention property.
3. We needed more time. It took a full five days to build a home. And although we had four teams, three were building homes and the fourth was putting an addition on the church. We were already stretched far beyond what we usually do with construction, and now we were adding another project—and a rushed one at that. We weren't sure if it could be done, but our plan was to take one worker from each site and attempt to build a home in two days (even though we had three days left, we knew most of the next day was going to be taken up simply getting supplies and finding a piece of property).
4. We wanted to make sure we didn't do the "American" thing where we jet in, build a home, and jet out. So the plan was to make sure the church was in agreement with our plan, as well as to find out if Claudia's husband was on board. Our desire was to facilitate a relationship between Claudia's family and the church.

For a small group of eighth-grade students and a handful of adults with only three days left, this plan seemed impossible. Yet this is what we believed God wanted us to do. And in spite of the obstacles, we had peace. Without exception, everyone believed God stuff was going to happen.

DAY 3

The next morning I placed a hat on the breakfast table. "There's no pressure. You know what we talked about last night. Each of you has asked Christ what he would have you give, so just do that. The hat will stay on the table until the end of breakfast, and we'll let you know how much 'green' was raised before we leave for the church."

Breakfast was quiet that morning. Even somber. The reality of what we were expecting God to do had sunk in. If enough money weren't raised, the plan would be over before it got started. After breakfast, as one crew cleaned up and the other packed up, Tom and Mark counted the money. Before loading up the vans, everyone gathered around Mark. "This morning, God answered our first request. This small group gave $2,500!" Everyone went nuts—jumping, dancing, screaming, hugging—praising God in a genuine middle school manner for allowing us to join him in his God stuff.

As a side note, even now as I write, I have that lump in my throat because I know what these students gave up. On the last day of our trip, they knew they could shop 'til they dropped, and they also knew about all the cool stuff there was to buy. Older brothers and sisters had come home in years past with machetes, alpaca hoodies, knockoff Oakleys, tie-dye T-shirts, and bags full of other goodies. Some of our students gave up every cent of their shopping money, as well as their snack money for the trip home, just to be a part of the God stuff. If necessary, they would have sold their shoes, watches, and even asked their parents to break into their piggybanks and wire the money to Mexico. They were that committed.

When we arrived at the church, we sent a few people to the local government office to negotiate the property purchase. Another group went supply shopping. Everyone else worked on the projects we were already committed to doing, while I met with the church leaders and the family in need. Day three lasted forever and beyond raising the right amount of money, nothing seemed to be happening. We left at the end of the day with a bunch of building material piled in the church, two volunteers planning to sleep on the supplies to keep thieves away, and not a single word about property.

Once again, during our gathering time, we prayed. And before we finished praying, we received word that property had been purchased. Not just any property; God gave us a piece of property right next door to the church.

DAYS 4 AND 5

The final two days were two of the hardest workdays of my life. Yet they were also two very joyous days. Everyone knew we were experiencing God stuff. His hand was moving in and through us. Even eighth-graders could sense this was an extraordinary moment.

The night after our last day of work, we reflected back on the week. What God had done was incredible. Not only were we part of this unbelievable story, there were dozens, if not hundreds, of other stories that had taken place during our short five days. And although statistics aren't the only measure of success, I was amazed to discover that, in spite of all the time and effort given to this one family, the numbers in every other area were higher than previous trips. More kids were involved in VBS, more contacts were made through door-to-door evangelism, more teenagers had been involved in our sporting events, and more people prayed to receive Christ. There was even a buzz in the community. Other groups had been there, but something was different about this group.

I share this humbly, because as stated throughout this story, all of this took place in spite of me, not because of me.

GOD STUFF HAD BEEN HAPPENING

It's been 11 years since this mission trip, and I've stayed in touch with many of the students. Most are still devoted to Christ and impacting others with their lives, and many point to the Mission Mexico experience as being a key transformational moment in their spiritual development.

Yet as I have reflected back on this and other youth ministry experiences, I've come to one primary conclusion: These trips, on their own, are *not* difference makers. Remove any trip from a particular context, and you get a different experience. It's the context of the trip, and the context leading up to the trip, that cultivates an *environment* for God to change lives.

The Mission Mexico trip, for us, was a microcosm of what we had been nurturing for years within our ministry. It was an experience encompassing all the elements we valued day-in and day-out. What made it such a high-impact trip was that these ministry elements were placed in an intensely focused format. This created a unique space conducive to seeing God do what he had already been doing within our group, but in a more concentrated, dynamic fashion. In many ways, this trip simply showcased the God stuff that had already been taking place within our ministry.

POLAROID LEADERSHIP

> *Vision looks inward and becomes duty....*
>
> *Vision looks outward and becomes aspiration....*
>
> *Vision looks upward and becomes faith.*
>
> **—Stephen Samuel Wise**

For a number of years before this particular experience, God had been doing something within me. Before I explain, please understand I believe deeply held convictions evolve over long periods of time. In other words, what's articulated next wasn't as clear to me back then as it is today. Yet even then it was transparent enough that I could articulate two major convictions I had about making disciples of Jesus Christ among students.

First was the concept of "beginning with the end in mind." Stephen Covey's classic, *The Seven Habits of Highly Effective People*, was rather new back then, and the idea of imagining, from the beginning, what a healthy, disciple-making ministry should look like made sense to me. It also made sense that this is how I should live life—to imagine what would be most valuable to me at the end of life and use that as a frame of reference by which to measure everything I did. As Covey says, "Beginning with the end in mind is based on the principle that all things are created twice. There's a mental or first creation, and a physical or second creation to all things."[2] Looking back, I believe this "end in mind" concept of making disciples was a precursor to the term *missional living*. Years ago we didn't talk about being missional, but we did discuss what truly devoted followers of Jesus look like and how ministries could produce such students. Granted, *produce* can be taken as an assembly line word and probably shouldn't have been used, but at least we were attempting to think through purposeful ministry.

The second conviction I held at my core was the importance of *environmental ministry*—as in creating the right atmosphere in ministry. Early on I became convinced that I couldn't produce anything in people, so if spiritual transformation was going to take place, I had to clearly understand the difference between God's role and my role. In fact, I quickly came to the conclusion that not only couldn't I produce life-change, but that I wasn't even responsible for it. Transformation, plain and simple, was God's job. My role was to cultivate an environment conducive to God's disciple-making work within me and the students I served.

I constantly talked about this concept with our adult ministry team. We strategized ways to develop disciple-making environments; ones in which God was completely in charge of transforming students. Our role was simply to create space for God to do what he wanted to do. We talked about how we could live out disciple-making principles in our own lives and establish an engaging model for students to follow. I believe this environmental idea was a precursor to the concept of missional living. While we didn't use the word, our environmental conversations were all about being missional.

There's one other word I didn't use back then, but I wish I had because it would've illustrated how these two convictions complement each other. What's more, it would've been a vivid illustration for that period of time—the BDC era (Before Digital Cameras). I've mentioned it previously in these pages. The word is *Polaroid*. Cheesy, I know, but the process of taking a Polaroid picture is exactly how I want to live life and lead ministry. Think about it:

- *To begin with the end in mind* is to focus on what you believe God wants your life and ministry to be about. Once you have clearly zoomed in on that mental picture—click.
- *Cultivating an environment* conducive to God transforming lives is like the process of all the colors and chemicals coagulating over time to bring the Polaroid picture into focus. It's the second creation (the physical creation) of the first creation (the mental creation).

POLAROID MINISTRY

The youth ministry I led used an acronym to help us articulate the disciple-making picture we wanted to create. The acronym finds it's meaning in another ministry story shared in the next chapter—the story of Jesus and the early church.

The acronym is ACTS. In my mind, it's the ultimate Polaroid of what a disciple-making ministry should look like. Why? Because it clearly paints the picture of disciple making, and it offers the environmental elements that must gel in order to cultivate such a ministry. In other words, it represented everything we wanted our ministry to be about:

- **Adoration.** An environment where Christ is worshiped, exalted, and adored. Adoration is not just an act; it's a lifestyle that's fleshed out in expressions of prayerful dependence, deep gratitude, and expectancy of what God can do. The focus of adoration is *upward*, to God.
- **Community.** An atmosphere of genuine caring, authentic relationships, and unity based on Christ's love for his church and his disciples' love for one another. The focus of community is *inward*, toward one another within the body of Christ.
- **Truth-and-Grace.** A setting in which God's Word is central to belief and behavior. It's the standard, the basis of everything taught and valued. The focus of truth is *downward*, from God. It's God graciously revealing truth to his people.
- **Serving-and-Sharing.** Serving isn't a project; it's a way of life. It involves helping the whole person. It means contextually ministering to both believers and nonbelievers by meeting their needs, as well as by verbally sharing God's message of grace. The focus of serving and sharing is *outward*, from the body of Christ to others.

This was the disciple-making picture I painted for our team and the picture our team strived to bring into focus. Back then we used phrases such as "begin with the end in mind" and "environment." Today we'd probably use the term *missional*. No matter what words are used, the concept is about being a disciple of Jesus Christ and joining him in his transformational work of making disciples.

POLAROID MISSION TRIP

Ralph Waldo Emerson once wrote, "People only see what they are prepared to see."[3] I believe this is why the Mexico Mission experience was merely a microcosm of what our ministry was already all about. Granted, it was a focused and intense experience, but it wasn't anything more than our group fleshing out what we were already doing. God stuff had been happening day in and day out within our ministry, and the Mexico trip just shone more light on it. Our students had been preparing for two years, and when the Mission Mexico experience rolled around, they saw God do his thing in a very vivid way. Consider what happened during that trip:

- **Adoration.** God was worshiped and exalted during this trip. And the adoration wasn't just a performance; it was becoming central to our lives. Adoration was fleshed out in prayerful dependence, as well as in a hope-filled expectancy for the God stuff we believed was going to happen.
- **Community.** Our group members genuinely loved and cared for one another. Although this sense of community had been growing for a couple of years, the Mission Mexico experience gave us a unique chance to flex our community muscle. We not only worked side-by-side, we also discerned together, through prayer, what we believed God wanted us to do. Then, we leaned on one another for the faith to believe God would actually do what, in our minds, was impossible.

Each environment has its own signature.

—Stephen Hopkins

- **Truth-and-Grace.** For two years we taught students the truth of God's Word. Even more, during the previous three months of extensive training for this trip, we reexamined many of the truths we'd previously taught. Then, during the trip, we were put in situations where we had to make a choice to either live out these truths or reject them. This was true even for me in the area of confessing sin. And although my leadership skills at the beginning of the week were lackluster, God's grace gave me the chance to model true confession. True confession might have been the most powerful leadership lesson these students ever learned from me (or, should I say, learned in spite of me).
- **Serving-and-Sharing.** Our team impacted many people, but it was the opportunity to holistically meet the needs of one family that changed us most. For several students this experience moved the idea of serving from a project to a way of life. They returned authentic disciples, actively engaged in God's work of making disciples among the nations, and they started by serving and sharing with their own friends.

I recently had a conversation with a Mission Mexico student who's now a young professional. As I talked with Keith and his wife over dinner, he shared how shocked he was to discover that practically every student at the Christian college he had attended was clueless about disciple making. "There was a unique disciple-making tone in our youth group that must have been missing in most other youth groups," he said. "Because of that, being a disciple who wants to join God in his transformation work of making disciples is just a part of my DNA. When I went to a Christian college, I thought the place would be filled with students who were serious about missional living, at least as serious as the key student leaders in our group. Instead, college was filled with people such as those who just attended our church services on Sunday mornings. I was shocked."

Looking back, I don't think I talked much about an ACTS environment with students. It was a tool I used with adult leaders, not with students. Even so, Keith got it. He understood principles such as beginning with the end in mind, environmental ministry, and missional living. In a nutshell, he knew what it meant to be a disciple committed to joining Jesus in his transformational work of making disciples.

GOD STUFF CAN HAPPEN FOR YOU

Yes, God stuff can happen for you and me, but hear this loud and clear: *You and I cannot make it happen.* Remember, transformation is totally in God's court; we're just responsible for serving up the environment. But because we serve a good God, I have faith that if you cultivate an ACTS environment in your ministry, you too will be telling God stuff stories for his glory.

Before taking a closer look at the basis for the acronym, let me share five things I love most about it. First, it's based on **Scripture**. More specifically, it's based on the early church as described in the Gospels and the book of Acts. (More on this in a moment.)

Second, it's **simple.** As I wrote in the introduction, early in ministry I hopped from conference to conference and resource to resource in an attempt to find a magic plan—the perfect approach to making disciples among students. Yet each time I stumbled on a new idea I liked, I simply added it to what I was already doing. Within a few short years, my ministry had become so complicated that volunteers needed a Ph.D. in physics just to decipher the code. Something happened, however, when I started understanding the acronym. Everything I held as important in ministry started to fit within these four elements. What I'd made complex was actually simple. Not simpleminded or effortless, but simple. Complete...comprehensive... simple.

Third, it creates **focus.** The essence of good leadership is knowing how to narrow the focus of those you lead to what matters most. Therefore, a movement or organization becomes stronger when the leader reduces the scope of the mission to its core elements. Why? Because a movement can't stand for something when it tries to be everything. It helps youth workers narrow in on the true scope of ministry. It says, "Here are the four things a disciple-making ministry should be about."

Fourth, building on focus, it's also **progressive**. It's alive and growing. It's that Polaroid thing I keep mentioning. As you'll see, one of Jesus' roles while on earth was to cultivate a movement called the church. The church didn't just happen. It developed and grew over time, but it started with Jesus. It's as if Jesus had a picture in his mind of what the church should be, and then throughout his ministry, he cultivated an environment that allowed that picture to congeal.

Finally, it fits any **context**. Please understand, though: I'm not contradicting what I said in the introduction about a one-size-fits-all approach; ACTS is actually much bigger than that. It's the core or essence of ministry, so it fits any ministry plan, no matter if a ministry is purpose-driven, Sunday-school championed, seeker-focused, or small-group centered. In fact, after discussing ACTS with thousands of youth workers all over the world, I have yet to find one who says, "No, it doesn't fit our context."

So have faith. You will tell similar God-stuff stories. In fact, soon you will not only be saying, "God stuff is going to happen," but "God stuff *is* happening."

THE ART OF ENVISIONING—POLAROID STYLE

Vision without action is merely a dream.
Action without vision just passes the time.
Vision with action can change the world.

- Joel A. Barker -

I'm convinced the reason more God stuff isn't happening in youth ministry today is that most ministry visions are underdeveloped. Don't get me wrong: Tons of youth workers are dreaming about God stuff. But their dreams aren't becoming reality. Either they don't have the right picture, or if they have the right one, they're not sure how to develop it.

To make matters worse, most youth workers I know are really trying hard. Their vision cameras are jammed with resources and ministry strategies, yet their film is producing underdeveloped prints. Is there a place youth workers can go to find accurate vision prints of what a disciple-making ministry looks like, as well as clues for how to develop these prints?

Absolutely.

Clearly developed snapshots of a disciple-making ministry are found in the story of another ministry—the ministry of Jesus. However, Jesus' finished prints are easily missed. Many mistakenly look to the Gospels for Jesus' vision pictures; but it's the book of Acts, not the Gospels, that gives the best final prints. The Gospels are like Jesus' Polaroids still developing. It's the book of Acts that gives the finished pictures—prints that are fully developed after all of Jesus' endeavors have gelled. Therefore, to truly understand

SOMETHING TO THINK ABOUT

Polaroid-style envisioning doesn't ignore the Old Testament or the rest of the New Testament. It simply zeroes in on the story of the early church as found in the Gospels and the book of Acts and attempts to learn from these stories.

The stories and instructions found in the Old Testament are still important to building disciples because they are part of the story of God. The Epistles are also important because they instruct the body of Christ regarding how to live. Finally, Revelation is important because it tells about the future of God's story.

Therefore, the whole counsel of God is important in making disciples. But when it comes to Polaroid-style envisioning, focus is important. And the focus is on the historical books in the New Testament that tell the story of how Jesus started his church.

Jesus' ministry, youth workers must learn the art of envisioning, Polaroid style.

More specifically, Polaroid-style envisioning looks at the Gospels and the book of Acts, not as two different stories, but as one. It recognizes that Jesus, from the beginning, envisioned what his group of ragtag followers could be (i.e., the strong believers found in the book of Acts), and this vision thoroughly influenced how he lived and led. Hence, Polaroid-style envisioning takes a picture of the finished, full-blown, disciple-making ministry found in the book of Acts (click), then moves through the Gospels to discover the key environmental elements Jesus cultivated in his earthly ministry that caused this picture to come into focus. Remember, "All things are created twice. There's a mental or first creation, and a physical or second creation to all things."[4]

First, one must begin with the end in mind by having a clear vision of what a disciple-making ministry looks like. This picture needs to be as focused as possible, which means all the elements should be vibrant, clear, and colorful. The book of Acts, specifically

Acts 2:42-47, gives such a picture. Second, each crystal-clear, vibrant element of the photo plays a role in seeing the vision become reality. These elements act as soil and seeds in the transformational environment that, over time, cultivates the vision.

That's it—Polaroid-style envisioning in its simplest terms. A cheesy term, perhaps—but a powerful concept.

SOMETHING ELSE TO THINK ABOUT

Ever notice how the Great Commandments and the Great Commission, as well as Acts 2:42-47, get more recognition than other passages in the Gospels and the book of Acts? If so, ever wonder why?

It's not because they're more important; it's because they're summary statements. The Great Commandments are Jesus' summary of the Old Testament. The Great Commission was Jesus' "commencement address" to his followers, which summarized what he had equipped them to do and challenged them to go and do it. Acts 2:42-47 summarizes what was happening in the early days of the church.

So don't buy into the claims that the Great Commandments and the Great Commission are the most important things Jesus said. Instead, view them as summary statements of all the important things Jesus said and did.

JESUS' PRIMARY MISSION

Before diving into the 101 practical ideas, we should discuss some foundational principles of Jesus' ministry.

For years I was taught, as you probably were, that Jesus' earthly purpose was to save the world from sin. "For God so loved the world that he gave his one and only Son, that whoever believes in him shall not perish but have eternal life" (John 3:16).

Then I was challenged with the idea that

Jesus' primary purpose on earth was to make disciples. This suggestion was based on the Great Commission. Before ascending to heaven, Jesus said, "All authority in heaven and on earth has been given to me. Therefore go and make disciples of all nations, baptizing them in the name of the Father and of the Son and of the Holy Spirit, and teaching them to obey everything I have commanded you. And surely I am with you always, to the very end of the age" (Matthew 28:18b-20). The notion was that everything Jesus did—his sinless life, his fulfillment of prophecy, his death and resurrection—was focused on cultivating a disciple-making movement. Therefore, Jesus' purpose was to make disciples.

Then, after more study and scrutiny, I've come to another conclusion altogether.

From a cursory study of the Gospels, one could argue that Jesus had multiple purposes while on earth. For instance, Jesus himself said he came:

- "To seek and to save what was lost" (Luke 19:10).
- To "proclaim the good news of the kingdom of God to the other towns also, because that is why I was sent" (Luke 4:43).
- Not "to abolish the Law or the Prophets...but to fulfill them" (Matthew 5:17).
- Not "to bring peace on earth...but division" (Luke 12:51).
- Not "to be served, but to serve, and to give his life as a ransom for many" (Matthew 20:28).
- "I was sent only to the lost sheep of Israel" (Matthew 15:24).
- "For this very reason [crucifixion] I came to this hour" (John 12:27).

Pick a purpose, any purpose, and I have heard a plethora of reasons why that one particular purpose Jesus spoke of is more primary than the others. Yet how can anyone make such a claim? For instance, how could one argue that proclaiming the good news is more primary than fulfilling prophecy? Or that seeking non-Christians so God may save them is more primary than serving and giving his life as a ransom for many?

On one particular evening, after a two-hour discussion with a mental gymnast and cerebral somersaulter compared to me, I had enough. It was time to settle this issue once and for all: *What was Jesus' primary purpose? Was it disciple making? Was it saving the world? Was it a combination of the two?*

I needed something I could get my theological arm and my pragmatic arm around at the same time.

In my study, I looked at many verses such as the ones mentioned earlier and noticed an overarching pattern beginning to develop. Scripture seems to teach that Jesus, while accomplishing many things and fulfilling many roles, had one overarching purpose: *To glorify his Father by doing the Father's will.* This is especially seen in the book of John:

> *Where there is no vision, there is no hope.*
>
> **—George Washington Carver**

- "My food...is to do the will of him who sent me and to finish his work" (John 4:34).
- "I tell you, the Son can do nothing by himself; he can do only what he sees his Father doing, because whatever the Father does the Son also does" (John 5:19).
- "For I have come down from heaven not to do my will but to do the will of him who sent me" (John 6:38).
- "I do nothing on my own but speak just what the Father has taught me...I always do what pleases him" (John 8:28-29).
- When predicting his death, Jesus talked about wanting to be saved from "this hour," but then told his Father that his life is about one thing: "Father, glorify your name!" (John 12:28).
- "The words you hear are not my own; they belong to my Father who sent me" (John 14:24).
- Before going to the cross, Jesus said, "I have brought you glory on earth by finishing the work you gave me to do" (John 17:4).

Jesus' purposes and roles (e.g., preaching the good news, seeking and saving, fulfilling prophecy, living a perfect life, his death and resurrection, and even disciple making) all fall under his overarching mission to fulfill his Father's plan; and since Jesus' mission was to do the will of the Father, he accomplished the plan.

Perhaps nowhere in Scripture is this seen more clearly than in Philippians 2:6-11. When speaking of Jesus, Paul writes:

> Who, being in very nature God, did not consider equality with God something to be used to his own advantage; rather, he made himself nothing by taking the very nature of a servant, being made in human likeness. And being found in appearance as a human being, he humbled himself by becoming obedient to death—even death on a cross! Therefore God exalted him to the highest place and gave him the name that is above every name, that at the name of Jesus every knee should bow, in heaven and on earth and under the earth, and every tongue acknowledge that Jesus Christ is Lord, *to the glory of God the Father.*

JESUS' PRIMARY ROLES

Isn't this a 101 ready-to-use ideas book? What's up with all the theology stuff?

Good question.

Understanding the context of Christ's earthly ministry has ***everything*** to do with making disciples in your youth ministry context.

What's more, the clearer we are about what Christ did during his time on earth, the more elevated disciple making—and the role we play in the process—will be in our minds. So let's go just a bit further with our understanding of the life of Christ.

If Jesus' earthly ministry was about glorifying the Father, then everything Jesus did was for the purpose of doing the Father's will. Again, Jesus accomplished many things. He fulfilled prophecy. He lived a perfect life. He died and rose again. He made disciples. As a pragmatic theologian, I'm interested in how all these things fit together. Were there any primary roles Jesus played while on earth? I think there were. If one looks at all Jesus did while on earth, I believe everything can be categorized into two major roles: Jesus provided the *means* of redemption and cultivated a *movement* of the redeemed.

ROLE 1: THE *MEANS* OF REDEMPTION—PURCHASE

This first role is unique to Jesus. No other person could provide the means of redemption because no other person has been completely human and completely divine. Jesus' life, death, and resurrection provided the means for restoring the shattered relationship between humanity and the Godhead. He purchased salvation and justification for us. He paid the price to buy us back; a price no one could pay but him.

Most people see this as the primary purpose of Jesus' life. While it is indeed central, by itself it wasn't the complete will of the Father. There was more. And if Jesus accomplished this role, yet dropped the ball with his second role, God's grand plan wouldn't have been complete.

ROLE 2: THE *MOVEMENT* OF THE REDEEMED—PROCLAMATION

Not only did Jesus provide the means of redemption by purchasing it for us, he also cultivated a movement of the redeemed. The mission of this movement is simple: To live out the good news within the community of believers and share the good news with those outside the community of believers.

Now what I'm about to say is extremely important. Perhaps the most important thing I've written so far. Got your attention? Good.

It's essential to understand that Jesus' first role, providing the means of redemption, was fulfilled by Jesus. With his life, death, and resurrection, he *purchased* salvation and justification for us.

The movement of the redeemed, on the other hand, is not about *payment*. It is about *proclamation*. While we can't do anything to purchase redemption on our own, our words (i.e., what we say about Christ) and lives (i.e., our obedience to Christ) should proclaim redemption to others. While we had nothing to do with the means of redemption, we play a significant role in the movement of the redeemed.

> *Leaders establish the vision for the future and set the strategy for getting there.*
>
> **—John P. Kotter**

MORE THAN PRAGMATISM

This two-role view of Jesus' ministry, while simple and pragmatic, isn't just a means of forcing his ministry into some predesigned, easy-to-understand box. I believe these two roles are clearly seen in Scripture. They don't articulate everything seen in the life of Jesus, but they adequately summarize two significant roles he played to bring glory to his Father.

For instance, during Jesus' public ministry, it seems he spent as much time, if not more time, cultivating a movement rather than spreading the message himself. Early in his ministry he went from town to town sharing the good news about the kingdom, but by the second half of his public ministry, we see him pulling away from the crowds and spending more time with a few very committed followers. He even was saying things that were hard to swallow, and many turned away from him (John 6:60). Could it be that the beginning of his ministry was about gathering a following and the second half was about establishing that following?

Secondly, if Jesus' exclusive purpose was purchasing the means of salvation, why would he have even focused on followers? Why not get the message out to as many people as possible, as quickly as possible? Why not spend all three years traveling from province to province proclaiming the good news? Clearly he didn't follow this approach because his purpose included more than purchasing the means of salvation; he also came to establish a movement of the redeemed, known as the church.

Thirdly, if Jesus' life was only about purchasing the means of salvation, then the only thing needed to get the message out would've been a verbal witness. Obviously, while on earth, he would have been the primary mouthpiece for this verbal testimony, meaning he would have given every spare moment to proclaiming himself as the means of salvation. After his death and resurrection, however, if the only priority were vocally proclaiming the means of salvation, he could have put his angels in charge of sharing this message. Imagine Gabriel and a host of angels showing up every five to 10 years verbally proclaiming the gospel from the skies. Who wouldn't believe?

But Jesus' life wasn't just about purchasing the means of salvation. And it wasn't just about verbally proclaiming the good news. God's plan included more. God's plan included the establishment of a movement for proclaiming the gospel, both in *word* and *deed,* to the world. That's the true meaning of *proclamation*. It means giving a verbal *and transformational* witness, and it's the reason Jesus' proclamation movement comes by way of redeemed people. If the message is redemption, the best ambassadors are those who've been redeemed. This means that, practically speaking, the movement is as important as the means, because the movement is made up of people who have been transformed by the means.

OUR MISSION AND ROLE

Christ's earthly ministry has *everything* to do with making disciples. It elevates both disciple making and the role we play in the disciple-making process. We, and the youth ministries we lead, are part of a movement called "the church." This movement is all about proclaiming, through word and deed, that redemption is available. And at its heart, this transformational movement is a disciple-making movement.

> *You are a product of your environment. So choose the environment that will best develop you toward your objective. Analyze your life in terms of its environment. Are the things around you helping you...or holding you back?*
>
> **—W. Clement Stone**

When looking at our mission and roles, we can learn a lot from Jesus. Our mission is the same as his: *To glorify God.* And just as he had roles to play, we do, too. First and foremost, we are to be proclaimers of Christ. Again, this proclamation isn't only verbal. If God's plan had only called for a verbal witness, he could have employed a much more efficient means of spreading the word. But his proclamation plan includes evidence of transformation, so his ambassadors must be transformed people. That's us. We, the redeemed, get to share the good news of redemption. We've been commissioned to make disciples.

This is likely why Jesus' last words to his followers were words that called them to embrace the movement. "All authority in heaven and on earth has been given to me. Therefore go and make disciples of all nations, baptizing them in the name of the Father and of the Son and of the Holy Spirit, and teaching them to obey everything I have commanded you. And surely I am with you always, to the very end of the age" (Mathew 28:18b-20).

Notice, even though all authority was his, Jesus still chose to use a movement of humans to be his ambassadors. Why? Because who's a better ambassador for redemption than the redeemed?

Also notice the movement isn't just about telling; it's about action. "Go...baptize...teach...obey." Not just words of proclamation—actions.

And what is the objective? To make disciples. In the original language, "make disciples" is the only imperative. All the other action words are participles describing how followers of Jesus are to fulfill this disciple-making command.

Finally, how do we know the movement will succeed? Because Jesus is with us "always, to the very end of the age." The one who purchased the means of redemption will always be with those who are part of the movement that proclaims redemption. He promises to be with disciple makers.

THE ROLE OF YOUTH WORKERS

Not only are we called to join Jesus in his disciple-making movement, we're also called to lead part of it. And we get to lead the most energized, enthusiastic, engaged segment of the movement—students. Carl Wilson, author of *With Christ in the School of Disciple Building*, has a plaque on his wall with the words from the late missionary R. Kenneth Strachan that reads:

> The successful expansion of any movement is in direct proportion to its ability to mobilize and involve its total membership in constant propagation of its beliefs, its purpose, and its philosophy.[5]

I can't think of any group more involved and mobilize-able than students. They are looking for something meaningful and real for which to give their lives. What's more, if a student becomes a disciple maker early on, the chances of her being a disciple maker for life are very, very high. I've seen it. I know plenty of former students, now young adults in their 30s, who're still passionately involved in this movement of proclamation—all because 15 years ago they bought into the idea of disciple making.

ENVIRONMENTS THAT CULTIVATE TRANSFORMATION

Now that the groundwork has been laid, the rest of this book focuses on the role of youth workers in leading disciple-making youth ministries. But instead of pushing steps or programs, we're going to zero in on environmental issues that cultivate a transformational atmosphere in youth ministry. The ACTS environment has already been described, and in the following chapters, we'll look closely at how Jesus cultivated, from very small beginnings, each element of the environment.

But for now, let's look at the finished picture. When Christ ascended into heaven, he left a frightened, confused movement. Yet on the day of Pentecost and thereafter, we see a dynamic, vibrant, exploding movement. What happened? Was it supernatural, or had Christ cultivated the right ingredients over the previous three-and-a-half years, and now all the elements of the Polaroid picture were coming into focus?

Actually, it was a bit of both. On the day of Pentecost, the Holy Spirit showed up, and all the supernatural things Jesus had promised in John 14, 15, and 16 came to pass. This is a vital part of the equation, but it's a part of the equation for another book.

The other part of the equation, the part this book is about, is the Polaroid picture. Yes, Jesus had cultivated the right ingredients during his public ministry. He had invested well in his followers, and they were now ready to be the movement of the redeemed. They understood their role in the disciple-making process, and from Pentecost onward, they were fully engaged.

What did Jesus' vivid, crystal-clear, fully developed disciple-making picture look like? Snapshots fill the pages of the book of Acts, but the clearest print is in Acts 2:42-47.

> They devoted themselves to the apostles' teaching and to fellowship, to the breaking of bread and to prayer. Everyone was filled with awe at the many wonders and signs performed by the apostles. All the believers were together and had everything in common. They sold property and possessions to give to anyone who had need. Every day they continued to meet together in the temple courts. They broke bread in their homes and ate together with glad and sincere hearts, praising God and enjoying the favor of all the people. And the Lord added to their number daily those who were being saved.

Although I believe it is most healthy to view the four elements (adoration, community, truth-and-grace, and serving-and-sharing) as merging together—in the same way a tie-dyed T-shirt's colors, while separate, bleed into each other. For the sake of a closer look, let's break down these verses according to the acronym introduced previously:

- **Adoration.** They were breaking bread together (most theologians believe this included the Lord's Supper) and praying, and everyone was filled with awe. They met together in the temple courts, presumably for worship. They praised God together.
- **Community.** They were devoted to fellowship. All the believers were together and had everything in common. They met together in the temple courts and in each other's homes. They ate together. They worshiped together.
- **Truth-and-Grace.** They were devoted to the apostle's teaching. God's grace and truth were expressed regularly through the observance of the Lord's Supper (breaking bread together).

They continued to meet at the temple, a place of worship and instruction.

- **Serving-and-Sharing.** They sold stuff so they could give to those in need. They enjoyed favor with all the people, likely because they lived as redeemed people. And God "added to their number daily those who were being saved." God was doing the adding, but the book of Acts clearly demonstrates that the believers were doing the proclaiming by word and deed.

What a vivid, crystal-clear, fully developed picture of a disciple-making ministry. It's the picture Jesus had in mind from the beginning. It was his first creation—his mental creation. Then everything he did with his followers during his time on earth helped bring this picture into reality. All the experiences, all the teaching, and all the interaction congealed together, over time, to create this disciple-making snapshot. That was Jesus' second creation—the physical one.

As youth workers, our role is the same. To create a mental picture of a disciple-making ministry and then cultivate it into existence.

TIME FOR ACTION

The Joel A. Barker quotation at the beginning of this chapter reads: "Vision without action is merely a dream. Action without vision just passes the time. Vision with action can change the world." I agree.

> *The vision must be followed by the venture. It is not enough to stare up the steps—we must step up the stairs.*
>
> **—Vance Havner**

These first two chapters have painted a couple of vision pictures for you, but now it's time to start cultivating a transformational environment. Together let's examine some specific actions Christ took, early on, to bring his vision into reality, as well as 101 ideas for doing the same in our contexts.

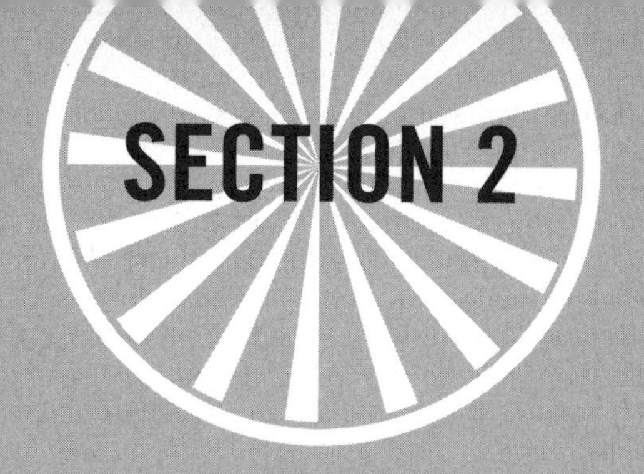

101 IDEAS FOR MAKING DISCIPLES IN YOUR YOUTH GROUP

Be careful the environment you choose for it will shape you.

- W. Clement Stone -

Equally important is to create an environment in which people can flourish.

- James Wolfensohn -

I planted the seed, Apollos watered it, but God has been making it grow. So neither the one who plants nor the one who waters is anything, but only God, who makes things grow.

- The Apostle Paul -

(1 Corinthians 3:6-7)

Note: *Section Two alternates between explanations and ideas. The first 25 ideas, which fall under the adoration umbrella, are preceded by a short section that sets up the ideas. Ideas 26 through 50 fall under the community umbrella, and they're preceded by a short section that sets up the ideas. Ideas 51 through 75 fall under the truth-and-grace umbrella, and they're preceded by a short section that sets up the ideas. Finally, ideas 76 through 100 fall under the serving-and-sharing umbrella, and they're preceded by a short section that sets up the ideas. (Idea # 101 is the Conclusion.)*

PREFACE TO PART 1

God is spirit, and his worshipers must worship in spirit and in truth.

- Jesus -

Adoration. Remember our environmental definition of *adoration*? An atmosphere of adoration in youth ministry fosters an environment in which Christ is worshiped, exalted, and adored. Adoration isn't just seen during singing or a service; it's championed as a lifestyle. This lifestyle is fleshed out in expressions of prayerful dependence, deep gratitude, and expectancy of what God can do. The environmental focus of adoration is *upward*, toward God.

Interestingly, Jesus' early disciples were more familiar with religiosity than adoration. How did Jesus move his followers from worship rookies to adoration champions?

CLICK—JESUS BEGAN WITH THE END IN MIND

First, let's get a clear picture of Jesus' fulfilled vision—a picture of these adoration champions from the book of Acts. We've already seen in Acts 2:42-47 that the early church worshiped God by celebrating the Lord's Supper, praying, meeting together, and praising him. Each of these is an *expression* of adoration. In other words, this is what the early church did to express their dependence, worship, and high esteem for God.

Yet the book of Acts is packed with many other examples of how the early church expressed adoration to God. They prayed, worshiped, sang, and rejoiced. But for simplicity's sake, let's look at the most common adoration practice of the early church—dependent prayer. Prayer is mentioned at least 34 times in the book of Acts. Check out some of the examples of how the early church prayed:

DON'T FORGET...

Each of the ingredients— adoration, community, truth-and-grace, *and* serving-and-sharing*—actually make a spaghetti together, so it's somewhat unnatural to separate adoration from the other ingredients. Even more, true adoration is more of a lifestyle than a stand-alone action.*

Why is it important to understand this?

Because practically everything else recorded in Acts 2:42-47 technically falls under the adoration umbrella. Fellowship, sharing with those in need, eating together, sharing the good news—each is an action taken by people who adore God, so each could be considered an act of adoration.

- "They all joined together constantly in prayer" (Acts 1:14).
- "After they prayed, the place where they were meeting was shaken. And they were all filled with the Holy Spirit and spoke the word of God boldly" (Acts 4:31).
- "They presented them to the apostles, who prayed and laid their hands on them" (Acts 6:6).
- "While they were stoning him, Stephen prayed, 'Lord Jesus, receive my spirit'" (Acts 7:59).
- "Peter sent them all out of the room; then he got down on his knees and prayed. Turning toward the dead woman, he said, 'Tabitha, get up.' She opened her eyes, and seeing Peter she sat up" (Acts 9:40).
- "I was in the city of Joppa praying, and in a trance I saw a vision" (Acts 11:5).
- "So Peter was kept in prison, but the church was earnestly praying to God for him" (Acts 12:5).
- "While they were worshiping the Lord and fasting, the Holy Spirit said, 'Set apart for me Barnabas and Saul for the work to which

I have called them.' So after they had fasted and prayed, they placed their hands on them and sent them off" (Acts 13:2-3).

- "Paul and Barnabas appointed elders for them in each church and, with prayer and fasting, committed them to the Lord, in whom they had put their trust" (Acts 14:23).
- "About midnight Paul and Silas were praying and singing hymns to God, and the other prisoners were listening to them" (Acts 16:25)

Wow! Their prayer was dependent, expressive, empowering, evangelistic...but most of all, expectant.

Expectant—I love that word. It communicates a sense of strong belief that God will do God stuff. And if there's one thing that can be said about the early church, its members were expectant.

What's astonishing is that their expectancy wasn't tied to circumstances. They expected transformational God stuff in good times and bad times; when the church grew, and when it scattered; while they had favor, and while they were being persecuted; and whether they were experiencing freedom or imprisonment. Sure, there were moments when their faith was lacking, such as when the church prayed for Peter's release. He showed up, and they assumed he was an angel. (I'm not sure which requires more expectancy—seeing Peter released from prison or seeing an angel.) Yet for the most part, their faith in God doing God stuff was demonstrated again and again by dependent prayer and—once their prayers were answered—by joyful celebration.

CULTIVATE—JESUS CREATING A TRANSFORMATIONAL ENVIRONMENT

What we see happening in the book of Acts finds its start in the ministry of Jesus. Remember, from the beginning, Jesus knew his group of ragtag followers would become the church, and this knowledge influenced how Jesus led them. In other words, the completely developed snapshot in the book of Acts has its simple origins in the Gospels (remember, Polaroid-style envisioning). Jesus lived, taught, and modeled adoration so that once he physically left this world, his disciples would know how to express adoration to God. Even more, they would know how to live it. This is why he cultivated an environment of adoration.

Look at that one aspect of adoration we examined earlier—dependent prayer. Jesus, the Son of God, saturated every aspect of his life and ministry with dependent prayer, and in turn, cultivated an environment of dependent prayer for his followers. One couldn't rub shoulders with Jesus for very long without realizing that adoration, expressed through prayer, was a staple of his spiritual diet. "His ministry began in prayer and ended in prayer. Over 45 sections of Scripture covering 30 events record how Jesus would often slip away to pray."[6]

Think about it—Jesus prayed during taxing times, before significant teaching moments, in the midst of excruciating trials, when following him was trendy, when he was rejected—the list goes on and on and on. What's more, the only teaching request the disciples made of Jesus recorded in Scripture is, "Lord, teach us to pray" (Luke 11:1). This points to the emphasis Jesus put on prayer.

Jesus also cultivated an environment of expectancy. At the beginning of his ministry he proclaimed, "The kingdom of God has come near" (Mark 1:15). Luke 4:32 says people "were amazed at his [authoritative] teaching." Jesus demonstrated to his followers, through teachings and miracles, that: "My Father is always at his work to this very day, and I too am working" (John 5:17). Even the new name he gave Simon—*Peter,* i.e., the rock—demonstrates Jesus' expectant vision he had for the church. As the early believers learned dependent prayer, they learned that dependent prayer moved God to do God stuff, and God stuff, in turn, led to more joyful, hope-filled expressions of adoration and expectancy.

YOUR TURN!

Just as Jesus' vision for the early church was fleshed out as he rubbed shoulders with his followers, so, too, will your vision be fleshed out. Remember, it was the everyday things Jesus did, over and over again, that cultivated the environment. Over time, the environment gelled.

In the next pages are 25 ideas to help you start cultivating an environment of adoration within your ministry. Remember, God transforms students; you simply cultivate the environment. Think of these ideas as seeds you plant in your group's soil. Water the seeds, cultivate them, and expect God stuff to happen.

And one more thing—the following ideas are only a place to start. Use them, but don't be overly dependent on them. If anything, let them spur you on to better, deeper ideas.

Adoration is caring for God above all else.

- Evelyn Underhill -

1. COMMON SACRED SPACES

Do you have a "special" place? A spot where you hang out, think well, or meet others?

One of my special places is Starbucks. I know, I know...if *special* means uncommon, Starbucks isn't unique. However, for 73.2 percent of all youth workers (statistics taken from my unofficial, unscientific, guesstimation), Starbucks is *the* place to write, read, think, meet friends, and oh yeah, drink coffee (I'm at a Starbucks right now as I type these words). There's a mesmerizing, magical force within that green logo that pulls us in. It's almost sacred.

Common places in our ministries can become special spots for students as well. The key is being intentional about creating "space" during regular programming where students can think about, write, and even hang out with God.

Allow these ideas to jump-start your brain as you think about creating sacred spaces during weekly programming, such as youth meetings, small groups, or weekend gatherings:

- *Space* doesn't necessarily mean square footage. After your next meeting begins (after everyone catches up with each other and grabs a few munchies), give students 10 or 15 minutes to write in prayer journals. One ministry I led did this with our small groups and even had students turn in their prayer journals to their adult leaders. Leaders prayed throughout the week for their small group members and wrote personal responses. After a few months—wow! We were astonished at the level of personal stuff students shared through prayer journals. Even more, our written responses allowed weekly opportunities for leaders to model Christ-like thinking and living to students.

- For an entire month, set up a prayer labyrinth in one corner of the youth room. Allow students to choose how they'd like to express adoration to God during worship time—within community or through individual expression. Let both group worship and individual labyrinth journeys happen simultaneously.
- Plaster an entire wall in the youth room with paper. At the top write *Talking with God* or *Wall of Remembrance*. Provide a different colored marker for each week and encourage students to write worshipful thoughts about God, answers to prayers, or questions for God. By the end of the year, the wall will be plastered with God stuff.

2. UNCOMMON SACRED SPACES

I have a second special spot that's more special (dare I say more sacred) and definitely more uncommon than Starbucks. It's any authentic sushi bar I can find. (If you're not a sushi connoisseur, you need to know something about us—we're unique...strange, bizarre, or insane...depending on your vantage point). Honestly, take a dash of wasabi, stir it with soy sauce, and we'll dip and devour practically anything. Plus, we pay big bucks to do it.

> *I never knew how to worship until I knew how to love.*
>
> —**Henry Ward Beecher**

Uncommon settings such as retreats, camps, and mission trips give youth workers uncommon opportunities to create sacred spaces. Try ideas like this during your next retreat or camp to establish an environment of adoration:

- During an extended singing experience, set up three stations in different corners of the room. Allow students to get up and go to these spaces whenever they please—even in the middle of singing. Since some teenagers will stay put and sing while others roam, worship might feel a bit random, so make sure the worship team knows what's coming. Each station should have a different feel to it, such as:
    - Station 1: Fill one corner with overstuffed pillows, beanbag chairs, journal notebooks, and pens. Encourage students to jot down thoughts about God or just scribble their feelings.
    - Station 2: In another corner, place standing tables with candles on each. A coffee bar can even be set up. Be sure adult leaders are at this station, making this the spot where students can go to chat quietly with someone about what's going on in their lives. Consider it an ongoing altar call area (minus multiple renditions of *Just as I Am*). This allows students to process aloud what God is doing in their lives *at the very moment God is doing it*.
    - Station 3: In the remaining corner set up tables filled with paper, paint, crayons, and sculpting clay. Allow students to adore God with shapes and color. No strict guidelines; just let them create.
- Here's a bonus idea: A few weeks after the retreat, take students to a reverent place such as a monastery or park and give them time to process two questions:
    - Question 1: *God, what are you doing in my life?*
    - Question 2: *God, how do you want to use this recent retreat to transform me?*

3. SLUMBER PRAYER PARTY

Host a lock-in for those ready to be stretched in their walk with Christ. While attendance might be lower than traditional lock-ins, remember success is not just about numbers. If promoted properly, those who attend will be prepared for a significant spiritual challenge, making success highly likely.

Once everyone arrives, provide each person with a white pillowcase and a colored, glow-in-the-dark, permanent marker. Use a different color for each student. Have each student write his name in the corner of his pillowcase.

> *To gather with God's people in united adoration of the Father is as necessary to the Christian life as prayer.*
>
> —**Martin Luther**

During the first two hours, mix interactive activities with teaching on the role prayer plays in obedience. Explain to students that one way believers express adoration to God is by relying on God, through prayer, to empower them for obedient living (Philippians 3:4-9; 1 Peter 3:8). Stress that real worship is demonstrated through obedient living more than through perfect singing, raised hands, or closed eyes.

After teaching, give students significant time alone to journal about their need for empowerment in obedience. Ask students to come up with a slogan or expression that will remind them to be prayerfully dependent.

When students come back together, have them sit in a circle with their pillowcases. Ask the students to pass their pillowcases to the person on their right and allow that person to write her slogan or expression on the pillowcase she just received. Keep passing the pillowcases until everyone has written on each. Once the pillowcases have made their way around the circle, each will have colorful, glow-in-the-dark prayer slogans all over them.

If time and space on pillowcases permit, let students slip away once again by themselves to write one or two short prayers on their own pillowcases. This will make the pillowcases more personal and powerful.

As a closing challenge, encourage students to pick a phrase from their pillowcases to reflect on and pray through each day of the next month. Remind them once more that real adoration is seen in how they live, not just in what they say or sing, and that picking a phrase each day will serve as a reminder of the importance of obedient living.

4. SINGLE-THOUGHT PRAYERS (A.K.A. "POPCORN PRAYERS")

This one is an oldie but a goodie—and works particularly well with middle schoolers.

Many students, especially when first entering youth ministry, don't know how to pray. If they're asked to pray aloud, they freeze. *What do I say?*

How do I say it? What if I use the wrong words? For some, it's a crisis so brutal that they choose not to come back to youth group.

Since prayer is such a key component of adoration, the ministries I've led always strived to teach students early on how to pray. From day one in middle school small groups, we end the evening in prayer. Additionally, we encourage every student to pray aloud. Our goal is to cultivate an environment in which every small group member can feel comfortable praying aloud by the end of the school year. One exercise that worked well was *Single Thought Prayers* (a.k.a., *Popcorn Prayers*). Its basic components include:

- **Explaining prayer** to students. Say something such as: "If you're a Christ follower, the Bible says you can 'approach God's throne of grace with confidence' (Hebrews 4:16) and even call God the Father 'Daddy'" (Romans 8:15 and Galatians 4:6). This means prayer is nothing more than having a conversation with God. While it shouldn't be done frivolously—it *is* a conversation with the Creator of the universe, after all—it also doesn't have to be fake or formal. God wants each of us to authentically approach, open ourselves up, and share our lives with him. (As an FYI, the healthy tension between the seriousness of prayer and the approachability of God might need explaining at this point.)
- **Explaining *Single-Thought Prayers*** as an easy way to learn how to pray aloud. A *Single-Thought Prayer* is exactly what it sounds like—praying about one thought at a time. It can be a praise, a request, a question, or even a statement to God. Tell students that most *Single-Thought Prayers* are a sentence or two in length, then give them a few examples.

> *Prayer is as natural an expression of faith as breathing is of life.*
>
> —Jonathan Edwards

- **Set-up guidelines.** Explain that students don't have to pray, but encourage everyone to give it a shot. Remind them that this group is a safe place and an ideal environment to learn how to pray. Also, be sure students realize each person can pray more than once, and that prayers should last for no more than a minute.

- **Describing the benefits.** With middle schoolers I often call this approach "Popcorn Prayers" to give them a visual for how prayers should pop from one person to another. This name also describes the benefits of this approach. When someone prays, that person's prayer might "pop" a praise or request in someone else's mind and lead him to pray. Then his prayer "pops" a thought in someone else's mind. It keeps prayer fresh and moving.

5. ADORATION GOALS

Social scientists have done extensive research on goal setting. The basic conclusion: A person becomes what she thinks about most. Hence, most social scientists champion writing and reviewing goals as a proactive way to think about what matters most.

Ever consider helping students write adoration goals? It's a great exercise, especially for small groups. Here's how it's done:

- **What?** Have students list one or two things they'd like to see happen in their walk with Christ in the next six months. Don't let them write "Do more Bible study" or "pray more." Instruct them to focus on transformational issues such as "to care more deeply about non-Christians" or "to stop gossiping."
- **Why?** Have students write why they want to see this change in their lives.
- **How?** Be sure students understand they're incapable of making this change happen on their own (Romans 7), but they can do some things in their lives that cultivate environments for transformation. Teach them about spiritual disciplines and have them pick one on which to focus. Have them set goals for how they'll practice these disciplines.

By the way, setting goals is easy; regularly reviewing them so they turn into a habit is what's tricky. Help students do this by talking regularly about their adoration goals, asking questions about how it's going, sending encouraging emails or postcards, and sharing the ups and downs of your own adoration goals.

6. TALK UP EXPECTANCY

Do you talk to students about what you hope God will do in your ministry? In many cases, that's all it takes to build expectancy.

One youth pastor I know, who was leading a high school ministry of about 30 regular attendees, believed God was pressing him to pray their group would see 25 friends become followers of Christ. This youth pastor became convinced this desire was of God, so he prayed accordingly. Within a matter of weeks, he sensed the Holy Spirit directing him to tell students in the group about his prayers. "No way!" was his first response. "But I couldn't shake the conviction. It actually led to sleepless nights, and I felt that if I didn't tell students, I was being disobedient."

When he couldn't take it any longer, he shared his thoughts. He asked his group to pray about it as well and report back. During their next weekly meeting, after much discussion, everyone was in agreement. Each person believed God wanted to use their group to reach 25 friends.

"We were excited, but also petrified. We knew it was humanly impossible to reach 25 students. I'd been at this church for five years and had never seen more than a handful of students commit their lives to Christ during a single year. In fact, we hadn't seen 25 students choose to follow Christ during my first five years combined! If it was going to happen, it was going to be a 'God thing.'"

"And a God thing it was. Exactly 25 students committed their lives to Christ during that school year. Amazingly, the group didn't do any extraordinary programming to make it happen. They were more intentional about inviting friends and creating opportunities to respond during regular programming, but for the most part, everything else remained the same. What was different was their hope and expectancy. The students were dependent, and their prayers had a focus. Every time they got together, their conversations revolved around whether God stuff would happen. Then, when things started happening, momentum built. There was a snowball effect—the more God did, the higher their confidence grew. Their hope moved from human-based hope, as in, 'We hope it happens,' to divinely inspired hope, as in, 'It's a sure thing because God's behind it.'"

"That year forever changed the lives of students," says this youth worker. "And it wasn't slick programming or a special event that did it. It was an encounter with God."

This youth pastor's only word of advice: "Do NOT manipulate students. Don't create impossible goals out of thin air just to get everyone excited. You must truly believe you're hearing from God before laying out an impossible challenge. At the same time, however, if you sense God directing you, don't keep quiet. Nothing transforms students like an encounter with God."

7. TOUR DE PRAYER

An occasional change in the physical environment of a group meeting can go a long way toward cultivating an environment for dependent prayer. So consider loading students up and taking them prayin'. Here's how it works:

- Depending on the size of your group, line up the appropriate number of vans or buses.
- Once students arrive, load them up and take them to three or four locations around town. The idea is to go to places that will focus their prayers. For instance, take them to a running track and have them pray about their personal walk with Christ. Take them to a school and have them pray for teachers, their principal, and classmates. Take them to a hospital and have them pray for the sick and needy. Take them to an airport and have them pray for missionaries. The list is virtually endless.
- Have a sheet of instructions for each site that includes how long you're staying, where they can go, and what they should pray about. Keep instructions short and simple; everything should fit on a 5 ½ by 8 ½ sheet of paper.
- Hand out each set of instructions as individuals get out of the vehicles at each location. Don't hand out all the instructions at the beginning of the evening; it will ruin the surprise factor.
- Instructions should lead students into dependent prayer. For instance, if you're going to a hospital, instruction sheets should first lead students to think about the pain that patients and families may be in. Second, they should instruct students to pray for the healing and restoration of all who are in the hospital. Finally, instructions should remind students that, in their own power, they can do nothing to transform others' health. Their role is to cultivate an environment that opens up deep friendships and spiritual conversations. The best step in cultivating such an environment is praying for God's Spirit to be at work.

- Vary how they pray at each site. For instance, have them pray privately at the running track. Have them pray with their small group at the hospital. Again, the potential for variety is practically endless.

8. TOUR DE PRAYER—HARD CORE

Want to make the Tour De Prayer idea extreme?

Turn it into an actual bike trek.

Set up a day bike trek that is 25 to 30 miles long or a weekend experience that is 50 to 75 miles. Each leg of the trip should be six to 10 miles. At each stop, have plenty of fluids and energizing food, but also take time to gather everyone together for focused prayer. Have students pray individually, pray in small groups, or pray as an entire group. Use variety to keep things fresh.

Also, before sending students off on the next leg, give specific prayer instructions for during the ride. For instance, have them pray between certain mile markers. Or ask them to pray during the first five minutes of the ride. And give them a prayer focus before releasing them on their way.

Finally, use this physical experience to get students thinking about dependent prayer. Connect the physical challenge of completing the trek to the spiritual challenge of prayer. For instance, talk about how encouraging each other while biking is similar to supporting each other through prayer. Teach how prayer's energy is similar to the physical energy gained through food and fluid. These make for memorable, hands-on lessons.

9. NON-VERBAL PRAISE

Play a popular worship CD during this experience. You'll also need several different-colored dry-erase markers and a large white board. As the music plays, instruct students to focus on something specific about God. It can be one of God's attributes, a personal experience they had with God this past week, or a particular passage of Scripture. The key is to get them focused.

Then say something like this: "During the next five minutes, we're going to worship God without singing or saying anything. I've passed out five different colored markers to students in the room. While the music is playing, I want these students to go to the white board and write a word or short phrase expressing adoration to God concerning *whatever you just instructed the students to focus on*. After these individuals write, they'll randomly hand the markers to others in the group and allow them to write. This process will continue for the next five minutes. Most of you will have several opportunities to write praises to God. Also, while waiting for a marker, read what others are writing. Let their words inspire your praise, perhaps even help you think fresh thoughts about God."

As the one leading this experience, keep two things in mind. First, it's especially powerful after teaching specific attributes of God. It'll give students a chance to authentically respond to what they've learned by praising God in a focused manner. It'll also help them cement what they've learned.

Second, allow time for the group to process the experience afterward. Let students discuss what just happened. Often you will hear comments along these lines:

- "That was powerful. I never realized I could worship God without singing."
- "When Steve wrote ____________________ about God, it made me think of ____________________________ . That's why I wrote those words on the white board."
- "What does the phrase ____________________ mean? I see it written on the board, but I don't quite understand."
- "Is God really _________________________________ ?"

Such comments open up deeper conversation about God, allow students to tell stories about what God has done in their lives, and give leaders great teaching opportunities. Moreover, the conversations often create an air of expectancy. Why? Because real conversations about a real God who does real stuff leads to students wanting to see this God do real things among them.

10. HOUSE GROUPS

For years, my wife, Kathy, and I have had both our small groups meet together at our home. She always has four to five girls in her group, and I have the same number of guys in mine. We call these combined groups a *house group*, and our house group always provides great adoration opportunities. If you're interested in doing something similar, here are some keys.

First, successful house groups require more time than typical Bible studies because they're community-oriented. For us, this means instead of having our gathering last the typical 90 minutes and consist of only Bible study and prayer, we're together for at least three hours. We start most nights with dinner. Then we hang out and catch up, have students write in prayer journals, and perhaps kick off the Bible study together. After this, we break into small groups (the girls with Kathy and the guys with me). Finally, we finish most evenings with prayer or community worship, followed by some more hangout time. All this extended time is huge in creating a community feeling among students (discussed in detail in the next two chapters), and leads to a willingness on their parts to express adoration to God more openly.

Second, if you tap into the house group approach, be sure the small groups don't lose their identities. This is especially important for personal sharing and prayer. If your house group is gender mixed like ours, it'll likely consist of about 10 students. In this group size, a few individuals will dominate all personal sharing and prayer if you let them (usually the loudest and/or neediest). However, you can use the small groups within the house group, especially if they are gender specific, for deeper sharing and prayer. Even more, praying aloud won't be limited to only those confident enough to pray in a larger, mixed context such as the house group. Even shy students will likely feel comfortable praying aloud with their small group once trust is developed.

Third, although it's important to keep small groups distinct, be sure to take advantage of the built-in variety that house groups lend. For instance, singing together usually feels weird for a group of four or five (especially four or five guys); but in a group of ten, it's much more natural. And the *Non-Verbal Praise* exercise described earlier works much better with a mid-size group than with a small group.

11. HOT TUB PRAYER

Granted, this one may sound a bit different, but it works...so stay with me.

I have a hot tub built into my backyard deck. Pretty cool in and of itself; but I've discovered it's an awesome ministry tool as well, at least for guys. The guys in my small group love ending a meeting night in the hot tub. What's most interesting is our conversation frequently ends up being deeper than if we were sitting on sofas or huddled around the kitchen table. I'm not sure why; perhaps it's because we're relaxed, or perhaps there's just something magical about being outdoors, at night, in the middle of winter, looking up at the stars while sitting in 104-degree bubbling water. Whatever the case, deeper conversation and authentic prayer occur more often in my hot tub than practically any other place. Go figure.

Don't have a hot tub in your backyard? You might still be able to tap into the hot tub magic. If a member of your small group has one, invite yourself over (tactfully, of course). And even if you can't find hot tubs in students' backyards, not all is lost. During certain retreats or conferences, such as ministry trips or small group retreats, hot tub prayer works well.

Before trying this idea, a word of caution: I've never seen this work in mixed groups. Let's be honest; prayer isn't likely at the forefront of the typical teenage guy or girl sitting in a hot tub with members of the opposite sex. So don't be disappointed if, during your next retreat, the guys and girls who always make their way to the hot tub during free time aren't too excited about your impromptu prayer meeting. Single-gender hot tub prayer is always the best idea.

One other word of caution: Never do hot-tub prayer one-on-one with a student, even if it's a same-gender student. (In fact, don't get into a hot tub with any student alone.) Being overly cautious, in this case, is prudent.

And a word of advice: This approach works best in quiet settings with smaller gatherings. This is one reason it works so well at my house. My neighborhood is quiet, and our group is small. And as hinted at above, it will work during the right kind of events. You probably don't want to try it at your next outreach retreat when 40 people are splashing around in the 6x6 foot hot tub, but a smaller setting such as a ministry team retreat would probably work great.

12. INDIVIDUAL PRAYER PATH

Popular ministry tools available on the market today are Prayer Paths and/or Prayer Labyrinths. These individual journeys guide people through hands-on adoration experiences such as reflection, prayer, devotional reading, and journaling. Most are self-guided via CD, and the few I've been exposed to are excellent. But if your ministry budget doesn't enable you to purchase such a tool, or if you intentionally want to go low-tech, try something like this:

- Cut out colorful arrows or footprints and lay them around your youth room to create a "path."
- Design stations along the path that have a different prayer focus. Some of the focuses could be:
    - Station 1: Have a map or globe with instructions to pray for missionaries or persecuted believers in particular countries.

- Station 2: Place notebooks here and have students write anonymous prayers to God.
- Station 3: Plaster a section of the wall with paper. Have students write on the wall the names of people who have positively impacted their lives for Christ, then have them spend a minute praising God for bringing those people into their lives.

> *The life of prayer! Great and sacred theme! It leads us into the Holy of Holies and the secret place of the Most High. It is the very life of the Christian, and it touches the life of God.*
>
> **—A.B. Simpson**

- Station 4: Have MP3 players and headphones here. Download one worship song that repeats itself over and over in each MP3 player. Print out copies of the lyrics so students can read along while they listen to the song. Instruct them to reflect on the words and present them back to God as an expression of praise.
- Station 5: Provide one notepad of paper and ask students to write down a single prayer request on the pad. Then ask them to pray for their request, as well as others written on the pad.
- Station 6: Place 3x5 cards at this station and instruct students to each write the name of one non-Christian friend on a card. Have them pray for their non-Christian friends, then place the 3x5 card into a shoebox. Use the shoebox of cards at the end of the night, as well as during future meetings, as a reminder for students to pray regularly for their friends.
- Station 7: At this last station, plaster the wall again with paper. This time, however, instruct students to write an attribute of God they appreciate, along with a simple sentence that describes why. It might be helpful to have a poster at this station with the names and descriptions of the attributes of God.

- Wrap up the evening by bringing everyone together for corporate worship through singing and prayer.

13. CORPORATE PRAYER PATHS

I took the individual prayer path idea and asked a friend of mine, Troy Hatfield, to create a "corporate" prayer path for about 30 youth workers at a conference I led. We divided everyone into six groups of five people each, appointed a facilitator for each group, had each start at a different station (each station was in a different room of a house), and rotate about every 15 minutes. It was a moving experience, and practically every youth worker took this idea home and recreated it for their youth group. Here's what we did.

- **FIGHT to hear the voice of God**: This room had an annoying CD of random noise playing, as well as a couple of TVs with static on the screens. We also had small journals for each person to write in and keep. The instructions read:
    - We reside in an aurally cluttered society. Noise battles for our attention. As people committed to being counter-cultural, we need to continually fight for space to listen for the whispers of God.
    - For the first three to five minutes, you are invited to battle the noise and seek to hear God's voice. Using the journal pages provided, take the remaining time to chronicle your experience. *Did you sense God speaking to you? How easy or difficult was this experience? What steps could you take to listen more intentionally for the voice of God on a regular basis?*
- **DEDICATE specific areas of life to God**: In the middle of this room was a large, rimmed plate with a couple dozen small candles on it. A couple of lighters were also available. The instructions read:
    - Often a physical act can move good intentions to true dedication. At this station, you are encouraged to move from the former to the latter in some areas of your life.

  - In what area of your life is God calling for higher commitment? Take time to consider the cost; ask yourself what it will cost to be obedient.
  - When you're ready, light a candle. Consider the lighting of the candle as an act of dedication, a declarative act of saying, "I choose to obey."
  - Notice how the candles begin to melt into each other. Consider how our choices to obey God are difficult, if not impossible, to separate from our connection with others. As each individual lights a candle, the connection between the candles becomes more vast and widespread. As a group, pray for each other, asking God to help each of you live obediently.

- **REMEMBER the sacrifice of Christ**: This room had communion elements available, but allowed participants the freedom to determine how to partake. The instructions read:
  - "Do this in remembrance of me." Familiar words. Words that grip us. Words that bring joy and celebration.
  - As a group, intentionally remember the sacrifice of Christ. Decide together how you would like to observe the Lord's Supper, then take time to bless each other, serve each other, and thank God for the amazing gift and selfless act of Christ.

- **EXPRESS love for the world**: This room was filled with maps, globes, and travel magazines. The instructions read:
  - The heart of God for the world is great. This same heart is what God wants to cultivate in his children.
  - Are there particular areas of the world or people groups for which God has burdened you? Write a prayer for them.
  - If you don't have a burden for a particular area or people group, ask God to move your heart to adopt a country or people group as a prayer focus.

- **CELEBRATE God's intimate and infinite love**: A chair and a full-length mirror were in the middle of this room. There were also several sheets of paper with portions of Psalm 139 written on them. The instructions read:
    - Scripture reminds us of the Father's amazing love. Too often this truth becomes theoretical and fails to grip our hearts. At this station take turns reading Psalm 139 to each other and take time to celebrate and revel in God's incredible heart for you. Be moved again by God's unspeakable love.
    - In turn, sit in front of the mirror. As you look back on your reflection, listen to the excerpts read from Psalm 139. Internalize the incredible truth of God's intimate and infinite love for you.
    - When the reading is finished, take time as a group to pray blessings into the life of the one seated. Pray that God's love would be real and transforming for that person. Pray that the closeness of God would bring a comfort and peace to his or her life.

  (By the way, this was the most emotionally moving station... grown men and women blubbered like babies because they realized in new ways how much God loves them.)

- **CELEBRATE the otherness of God**: There were two large tables in this room. One had paper, crayons, and paint on it. The other had mounds of sculpting clay. (There was tons of laughter at this station.) The instructions read:
    - We most often think and express ourselves through words and phrases, but we can also express ourselves through metaphors and artistic expression.
    - Be artsy at this station. Use the supplies provided to celebrate the otherness of God through some type of tangible expression—a drawing, painting, or sculpture. How has God demonstrated his unique character and person to you recently? Follow the example of our Creator and capture that experience in artistic form.[7]

14. DISTRACTION JOURNALS

Before any significant adoration experience begins, consider this idea. Have students find a quiet spot for some alone time with God. Don't let them take anything with them except a Bible, a simple journal you put together (three or four pages stapled together with an artsy cover will be fine), and a pen. Instruct them to get comfortable so they don't rush through this exercise. Explain that what they are about to do will help them focus on God.

> *A common problem, related to why we may seek to escape silence, is the discovery that it evokes nameless misgivings, guilt feelings, strange, disquieting anxiety. Anything is better than this mess, and so we flick on the radio or pick up the phone and talk to a friend. If we can pass through these initial fears and remain silent, we may experience a gradual waning of inner chaos. Silence becomes like a creative space in which we regain perspective on the whole.*
>
> **—Susan Annette Muto**
> ***Pathways of Spiritual Living***

Instruct them to open their *Distraction Journal* (i.e., the journal you create) and tell them to write, draw, color, or describe whatever might be keeping them from focusing on Jesus at that moment. As they doodle, instruct them to pray this prayer: "Jesus, please keep these things from distracting me. I want to be still before you."

After giving them 10 to 15 minutes, have them come back together for the adoration experience you have planned. However, let them keep their *Distraction Journals* with them. Tell them that at any time during the experience if their minds begin to wander, they can open up their journals and describe their thoughts. When they identify and express their distractions, tell them once again to pray that God will enable them to stay focused on him.

This exercise is great for three reasons. Obviously, it helps students deal with distractions during worship experiences. Additionally, it helps them identify the particular distractions they tend to face in everyday life. Finally, it gives them a tool to use on their own when distractions cause them to lose focus on God.[8]

15. VALENTINE'S JESUS

This is a great Valentine's Day experience.

Start by decorating the youth room with red and white balloons, streamers, hearts...the works. Set up tables with white linen, candles, and fine china. Have soft, romantic, but upbeat music playing.

When students arrive, have adult leaders escort them to their seats. For a stronger effect, have leaders dress elegantly (a tall order for most youth workers). Have an invitation at each place setting that reads: "I am head over heels, madly in love with you! Tonight, I want to show just how passionate I am about you. Love, Jesus." Let students help themselves to the snacks on the table, as well as talk to their friends, while they wait for the evening to start.

Once everyone arrives, play a few lighthearted Valentine's games or crowd breakers. The key at the beginning of the evening is to make things feel carefree.

After the games, have someone teach about the history of Valentine's Day for just a few moments (brevity is essential). Again, this should be lighthearted and fun. Afterward, transition by saying: "To celebrate Valentine's Day, we thought it would be appropriate to look closely at the one who loves us more than anyone ever could: Jesus. Let's see just how intense his love is for us."

Turn out the lights and show scenes from *The Passion of the Christ* (NOTE: Be sure to notify parents before using clips from this movie; it's rated R and brutally violent at times, and some parents may object). When the lights come back on, have adult leaders at each table ready to discuss what students are thinking and feeling. It would be wise to have questions prepared ahead of time that leaders process with students.

End the night by reading John 13:1-17, taking communion, and then reading John 19. Before taking communion, be sure students understand that the act of communion is perhaps the best way to express adoration to Jesus for all he has done for us.

One last thought: This would be a great way to kick off a series that explores the depth of Jesus' love.

16. SCRIPTURE PRAYER

An ancient style of prayer within Christianity is *Lectio Divina*, which stands for using the Word of God for prayer. This approach is not only a great method of prayer, but also helps students grow in their understanding of Scripture.

A group approach to using *Lectio Divina* is shared in Idea 69 of this book, but here's a simple approach to use in your personal life that can also become a powerful tool to equip students in prayer.

Select a favorite Bible verse and put it on a 3x5 card. Then, every chance you get, repeat it until it takes root in your heart. Repeat it when you get up, when you go to bed, while you are driving, when you are exercising, and when you are waiting in line for something. Additionally, take a verse or two each month that ties into your teaching theme and provide 3x5 cards with that verse on it for students. Encourage students to do what you are doing. Explain that praying Scripture back to God is like praying the very heart of God. It's bound to build confidence in those who do it, stretching participants beyond their normal prayer lives.

17. SILENCE IS GOLDEN

Teach students the art of silence. Give them two or three adoration passages from Scripture to ponder, and then let them wander. The only rule: They cannot say a word to anyone.

This works exceptionally well on a retreat, during a visit to a monastery or park, or even as a surprise at a weekly youth ministry program. You'll be amazed at how something so simple can be so powerful.

After 30 minutes or so, gather everyone back together and break into smaller groups. Have these small groups process the experience together. Ask questions such as:

> *Silence is nothing else but waiting for God's Word and coming from God's Word with a blessing. But everybody knows that this is something that needs to be practiced and learned, in these days when talkativeness prevails. Real silence, real stillness, really holding one's tongue, comes only as the sober consequence of spiritual stillness.*
>
> **—Dietrich Bonhoeffer**
> ***Life Together***

- Was it hard to be completely silent? Why or why not?
- Did you get distracted? If so, by what?
- Did you get more focused or less focused as time went by?

- What did the verse(s) cause you to think about?
- Did you gain any fresh insights about God? If so, what?
- How can you use this experience in your own life?

18. WALL OF THANKSGIVING

This adoration is great for the month of November.

Cover an entire wall in your youth room, or a large section of the hallway outside the youth room, with paper. Then, during each night of the month, give students time to write something for which they are thankful. Students can scribble pictures, write poetry, quote Scripture, or spell out a single word. Encourage teenagers to express themselves in ways that truly represent who they are.

Change the timing each night to keep this experience fresh. For instance, on the first night give students a specific time frame, such as the first 15 minutes of the meeting during hangout time. During the next night, allow students to get up anytime during your worship celebration. By the third evening, allow them to go to the wall any time. On the last night, use the wall as a way of responding at the end of the evening. By month's end, right around Thanksgiving, adoration pictures, phrases, and words to almighty God will fill your wall.

19. REAL-TIME GROUP PRAYER

God hears prayer in real time, even if every believer around the world is praying at the same time. One creative way to experience this reality is to have your entire group pray aloud at the same time. At first it will probably feel awkward for students; but when done in the right context, it's powerful.

Four thoughts:

- This usually works best with larger groups (at least 20 people or more) because most students will likely pray quietly at first. In a larger group, they won't be overly worried about people hearing what they're praying. Additionally, as a larger group begins to pray, the room will likely get louder as time goes on, which translates into more energy.

- Focus the prayer. Tell students exactly what you want them to pray about; this way they're not busy trying to decide what to focus on when the activity starts.
- Prepare your leaders, both adults and students, to pray aloud even if no one joins them at first. I once led this type of prayer without preparing my leaders, and I ended up being the only one praying aloud for what felt like an eternity.
- Consider using a creative group posture. For instance, I've asked students to form a circle, face outward, and hold hands while doing this exercise as a way of representing our group resistance to Satan's attacks and temptations.

20. REST RETREAT

> *Then, because so many people were coming and going that they did not even have a chance to eat, he said to them, "Come with me by yourselves to a quiet place and get some rest." So they went away by themselves in a boat to a solitary place.*
>
> —**Mark 6:31-32**

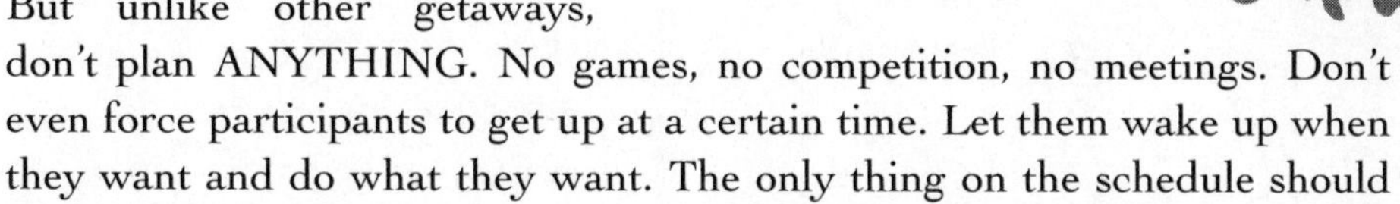

Students' live at 110 miles per hour. What's worse, we often step on their accelerators instead of helping them slow down. A *Rest Retreat* is a great tool for helping both leaders and students slow down and rest in Jesus.

Head to the mountains or a lake for a couple of days, just as you would for most retreats. But unlike other getaways, don't plan ANYTHING. No games, no competition, no meetings. Don't even force participants to get up at a certain time. Let them wake up when they want and do what they want. The only thing on the schedule should probably be meals (you don't want to drive your cooks crazy).

Students must understand the purpose of this retreat—it's to rest in the presence of Jesus. That's it. Therefore, encourage students to come only if they'll respect this guideline. Have them bring their Bibles, prayer journals, MP3 players (only if they exclusively listen to music that encourages them to focus on Jesus), and books to read. During the retreat, suggest walks, devotions, exercise, talking with friends, playing board games, praying, reading, journaling, or sleeping. Just be sure they understand that the point is to rest in Jesus.

THINK ABOUT IT...

Have you ever known students who regularly raise their hands or even cry during worship experiences, yet have serious patterns of sin running through their lives? I remember two such students. During worship celebrations, they'd raise their hands, fall to their knees, and shed tears. When asked why, they would say, "Because we're so moved." Yet immediately after the service, they would often sleep together. Even more, their actions and attitudes throughout the week didn't resemble true follower-ship.

These teenagers obviously had a wrong view of worship. They saw it as an emotional event that occurred once a week, not as a way of life. In reality, they were worshiping the event more than God. True worship always includes obedience. Be sure students under your care realize this truth.

21. PRAYER LABYRINTH

This is similar to the *Individual Prayer Path* described earlier but a bit more official and based on the Stations of the Cross. A Prayer Labyrinth is a maze with sacred prayer stops throughout. It usually employs interactive experiences, thematic art, and a host of other creative ideas. At each station, instructions need to be clear so students know exactly what to do.

For ideas on setting up your own prayer labyrinth, check out the article, "Walking a Sacred Path," in the November 1999 edition of *The Lutheran* magazine at www.thelutheran.org.

22. TAIZÉ WORSHIP

Taizé is a tiny village in the hills of eastern France and home to an ecumenical community of brothers whose prayer and reflection, three times a day, is central to their lives. From this humble setting, Taizé worship services have been spreading all across the world.

Taizé worship includes candlelight, prayers, silence, spiritual readings, and contemplative music (usually with repetitive words). The Lord's Supper is usually incorporated as well. Taizé services invite participants to meditate, be silent, and center on Jesus.

The Internet is packed with sites about this type of worship, and with a bit of research, you'll be able to develop a Taizé worship experience that fits your context. Just remember, this is a high-level adoration experience.

23. EMBRACE THE CHRISTIAN CALENDAR

Two friends of mine, Steve Argue and Dave Livermore, cofounders of www.intersectcommunity.com write:

> Sometimes the longest stretch in the youth ministry calendar can be that seemingly "dead zone" between the holidays and summer. Ironically, in the Christian calendar, this is the time of the year when everything heats up. It's called Lent and Easter. These days are the deepest, most significant, central part of our Christian existence. Lent and Easter are part of a greater rhythm called the Christian calendar that anchors us in a rich heritage of faith that has been the spiritual metronome of faith communities for hundreds of years...
>
> Lent isn't something that can just be squeezed in. Our youth ministry schedules won't allow for adding one more thing. But what if we let Lent shape our existing activities this season?
>
> For hundreds of years, Christians have emphasized two primary things during Lent: Turning from sin in repentance through denial of some of the things that so easily distract attention from God; turning to God by studying the Christian story and all it entails.
>
> Consider the following ideas for intersecting Lent with your ministry:
>
> - Be committed to Lent yourself. Study it, understand it, and do it.
> - If you regularly practice Lent, instead of the usual "chocolate fast," try fasting from the Internet at home for the next 40 days.
> - Read the Christian story that leads to the cross. Pick readings from the liturgical calendar (available

online) or pick your own readings that lead to Jesus' death and resurrection.

- Give up something together as a community. If it's something you regularly buy, turn in the money weekly and give it to a charity of your choice.
- Give your students Lent journals. Have them record their Lenten journeys and give them opportunities to share some of their discoveries along the way.
- Fasting reminds us of suffering. Read *Jesus Freaks*. Remind each other of the sacrifice of Jesus and of others who have gone before us.
- Remember, Sunday is never a fasting day because it's resurrection day. Find ways to create Sunday celebrations as a youth group community in the midst of your fasting.[9]

Think about it: By simply observing the sacred seasons of the Christian calendar, the adoration environment within your ministry can be revolutionized!

24. THE HOUR THAT CHANGES THE WORLD

A number of years ago Dick Eastman wrote a classic book entitled *The Hour That Changes the World*. In it Eastman suggests dividing an hour into 12 periods of five minutes each as a way to help people pray more effectively. I've used this approach with students dozens of times, and the results always have been powerful.

Outlines of this approach have been floating around for years. You can find one such outline at: www.jwipn.com/pdf/thehourthatchangestheworld.pdf. The following are the basics of what you'll find in this document:

1. **PRAISE**—Psalm 63:3, Hebrews 13:15, Matthew 6:9b
All prayer should begin with recognition of God's nature. The Lord's Prayer—our model for all praying—begins with "Our Father in heaven, hallowed be your name." Praise is that aspect of prayer that vocally esteems God for his virtues and accomplishments.

2. **WAITING**—Psalm 37:7, Isaiah 40:31, Lamentations 3:25
Not only should we begin prayer with praise, but time should be given to being quiet in God's presence. The original Hebrew text of Psalm 37:7 tells us to be still before God. This isn't meditation or just a time for listening; it's taking time to let God love you.

3. **CONFESSION**—Psalm 51:10, 11; 139:23, 24; 1 John 1:9
The psalmist asked God to search his heart for unconfessed sin. He knew that sin was one of the greatest roadblocks to answered prayer (see Psalm 66:18). Make time for confession early in prayer. This clears the way for powerful praying.

4. **THE WORD**—2 Timothy 3:16; Psalm 19:7, 8
"The commands of the Lord [God's Word] are radiant, giving light to the eyes," wrote young King David. When God's Word is brought into our prayers, we open our eyes to new possibilities in God. At this point in prayer, read God's Word.

5. **WATCHING**—Colossians 4:2
This is a time of spiritual observation—a time to be on the lookout for promptings from God and/or onslaughts from the enemy.

6. **INTERCESSION**—1 Timothy 2:1, 2; Psalm 2:8; Matthew 9:37, 38
Our prayer now centers on intercession for a spiritually dying world. This concerns praying for others who have desperate needs. Of course, intercession is one aspect of prayer where five minutes will never do. Usually half of my hour, or more, needs to be given to this aspect alone.

7. **PETITION**—Matthew 6:11; 7:7; James 4:2
This aspect of prayer concerns our personal needs. Petition is even included in the Lord's Prayer in the expression, "Give us today our daily bread." To petition God is to open our need to God through prayer.

8. **THANKSGIVING**—Philippians 4:6; Psalm 100:4
When Paul wrote to the Philippians, he instructed them to offer prayer and supplication "with thanksgiving." Thus, thanksgiving should occupy more than a single aspect of our prayer—it should be sprinkled throughout. Thanksgiving

differs from praise in that praise recognizes God for who God is, while thanksgiving recognizes God for special things God has done.

9. **SINGING**—Psalm 100:2; Ephesians 5:19; Psalm 144:9
Melody in its truest sense is a gift of God for the purpose of singing praises to God. Many Christians, unfortunately, have never learned the beauty of singing a "new" song to God during prayer. These songs may come straight from the heart with the Holy Spirit creating the melody. After all, Paul spoke of singing "songs from the Spirit" (Ephesians 5:19). To sing to God is to worship God in melody.

10. **MEDITATION**—Joshua 1:8; Psalm 1:1, 2; Psalm 77:12
To wait in God's presence is simply to be there to love God. Meditation differs in that during the latter our mind is very active. To meditate is to ponder spiritual themes in reference to God. In fact, only once in Scripture does God specifically promise success and prosperity, and according to the verse, these are God's gifts to those who meditate day and night in God's Word (Joshua 1:8).

11. **LISTENING**—Ecclesiastes 5:2; I Kings 19:11, 12
Whether through God's written Word or by the inner still small voice of his Holy Spirit, God speaks to praying Christians. Do you take time to listen? Listening is different from both waiting and meditation. Listening is the act of seeking direct orders from our heavenly Father concerning the activities of our day.

12. **PRAISE**—Psalm 100:4; Psalm 150
There's an imaginary door to every prayer time with a sign affixed to it that reads "PRAISE." We should always enter prayer through this door, and when prayer moves toward its conclusion, we must look for the same door. We begin our prayer by recognizing God's nature, and we end in similar fashion.

25. FROM ADORATION 101 TO 401

Cultivating an environment of adoration in youth ministry takes time. But time isn't the only issue. The intensity of each experience plays a role as well.

For instance, having teenagers learn to express themselves in prayer via Single-Thought Prayers is much less intense than having them participate in a Corporate Prayer Path. What's more, as an atmosphere of adoration develops within your ministry, there will be students at all ends of the worship spectrum.

Therefore, the best suggestion I can make to help you move both your ministry and individual students from Adoration 101 to Adoration 401 is to take a multilevel approach. This isn't some sort of pyramid scheme; it's just the most complete way of seeing adoration become part of the DNA of your group. To keep it simple, I'll again focus on how you can do this with one element of expressing adoration to God: Dependent prayer.

Outreach-level opportunities. Be careful of making outreach experiences so "seeker friendly" that opportunities for students to get a glimpse of authentic Christianity are forfeited. Look for chances to demonstrate how prayer is a natural, everyday part of following Christ. At our "attraction" and "get to know our group" events (events with no gospel presentations, where the only purpose is to expose our group to the community), we usually have a student share what she appreciates most about the group. At the end of this student's five-minute presentation, she prays a short prayer. The key is that this student always explains what prayer is by saying something such as: "For people who follow Jesus Christ, prayer is our way of sharing our thoughts and feelings with God. The Bible tells us that because we have a relationship with Christ, we can talk to God about anything. So I'm going to talk to God right now by saying a short prayer to thank God for this group and ask God to be real in all our lives during the next week." Simple, authentic, powerful.

Growth-level opportunities. These help students grow in their relationships with Christ. Common growth-level ministries include Sunday school, Bible studies, and small groups. A variety of prayer opportunities should be available for growth-level students such as:

- **Corporate prayer during every activity**. This can happen in a variety of ways, whether one person prays from up front or students break into groups to pray.
- **Regular teaching on prayer**. The best way to do this is to teach a series on prayer from time to time (annually or biannually), and to naturally include teaching about prayer in other series more frequently.

- **Prayer journals**. Incorporate prayer journals into small groups or create an MP3 self-study course on how to use a prayer journal.
- ***TAWG* resources.** The devotional material (e.g., *Time Alone with God* resources) your ministry provides should include a variety of prayer resources.
- **Adoration experiences.** Experiences such as prayer walks, concerts of prayer, and prayer stations should become a regular part of your growth-level programming. Don't get stuck doing the same thing every meeting. Adding just two or three of these experiences to your schedule will create variety for students and help foster an environment of expectancy.
- **Extended adoration experiences.** Adoration retreats, service projects, 30-Hour Famines, and other growth-level experiences should incorporate activities such as journaling, extended times of singing and worship, and prayer. These opportunities will help students dive deeper into prayer.

Ministry-level opportunities. These equip students to serve and reach out to others, especially peers. Obviously students at this level should be participating in the prayer experiences listed under the growth-level opportunities heading, so the need here isn't necessarily to provide more opportunities, but to teach them how to pray for others. Consider doing two things to focus their prayer:

- **Circles of Concern.** Trying to teach ministry-level students to pray for others can be difficult since once they get to this level, they begin to see the needs of students in their school, as well as the needs of people all over the world. This reality will likely feel overwhelming to them. To help them focus their prayer, use a strategy called Circles of Concern. Each ministry-level student lists two or three friends who don't have a relationship with Christ, two or three students in the youth group, and one overseas people group to make up their Circle of Concern. They're instructed to pray deeply about whom they believe God wants on their list, and then this list becomes their prayer and ministry focus. What's more, once they realize other ministry-level students are doing the same thing, they begin to see the power of this approach. By themselves they feel overwhelmed; but all the ministry-level students' efforts, taken together, can be revolutionary. During practically every ministry-level gathering, have students talk about and pray for their Circles of Concern.

- **Prayer Leadership.** Also ask your ministry-level students to set the prayer pace in the youth ministry. This means having the right attitude during corporate prayer, having a willingness to pray publicly, helping lead SYATP rallies at their schools, and championing prayer in their small groups.

BONUS IDEA: SUGGESTED RESOURCES

Remember, the ideas in this book are designed to jump-start your brain. Want to go deeper? Check out some of these resources:

- *The Book of Uncommon Prayer* (volumes 1 and 2) by Steven Case
- *Imaginative Prayer for Youth Ministry* by Jeannie Oestreicher and Larry Warner
- *Ideas Library* CD-ROM by Youth Specialties
- *Celebration of Discipline: The Path to Spiritual Growth* by Richard J. Foster
- *The Prayer Path: A Christ-Centered Labyrinth Experience*
- *Transformation Stations: Experiencing Jesus' Passion*

PREFACE TO PART 2

A new command I give you: Love one another. As I have loved you, so you must love one another. By this everyone will know that you are my disciples, if you love one another.

- Jesus -

Community. The working definition of *community* laid out in this book is an atmosphere where genuine, caring, authentic relationships are fostered, so that unity—based on Christ's love for his church and the love of those in the church for each other—can be established. In other words, the focus of community is *inward*—toward one another within the body of Christ.

When Jesus first started gathering followers, they resembled a loose group of individual brokers rather than a band of brothers. How did these men and women end up experiencing community to such a degree that they had everything in common (Acts 2:44)?

CLICK—JESUS BEGAN WITH THE END IN MIND

Let's again begin by getting a clear picture of Jesus' fulfilled vision of community—a picture from the book of Acts. In Acts 2:42-47 we see the early church developing community by devoting themselves to fellowship, being together, having everything in common, meeting together in the temple courts, and eating together in homes with glad and sincere hearts. Each of these was an *expression* of community.

Other examples of community in the book of Acts abound as well. Here's a sampling:

- In Acts 4:32-37, the early church was of "one in heart and mind." One way this unity was expressed was by believers sharing "everything they had" so that "there were no needy persons among them."

- In Acts 6:1-7, the apostles dealt thoughtfully and sympathetically with copious community issues such as cultural differences, leadership expansion, and caring for the needy, and they did so in such a way that the "proposal pleased the whole group" (verse 5).
- In Acts 8, the value of community was pivotal in how the Jewish believers handled new Samaritan believers. Christianity was exploding, moving outside Jewish boundaries, and this growth, if handled unwisely, could have spelled disaster for the movement. The Jerusalem church sent Peter and John to check out what was happening (wise move #1), and they recognized God's Spirit at work (wise move #2). They reported to Jerusalem (wise move #3), and the Jewish Christians accepted their new Samaritan brothers and sisters (wise move #4). This acceptance revealed how strong the bonds of unity were within the early church. What's more, this happened again with the Gentiles in Acts 10 and 11.
- To add to the latter point, the early church was multicultural before multiculturalism was all the rage. Jews, Samaritans, Gentiles, different nationalities...it was a melting pot. Yet the early church's solution wasn't separate sects; rather, they fostered community.
- During each major advance—from Jerusalem to Samaria to Antioch to the rest of the world—church leaders had to be creative, deal with criticism, and continue to cultivate community. This approach, if examined deeply, would constitute a comprehensive leadership study in just how important unity and a strong sense of community are in a growing movement. The early church couldn't have stayed unified without the work of the Spirit (remember: God transforms), yet the leaders of the early church played their roles well, cultivating an environment conducive to allowing God to develop community among believers.
- At the end of Acts, we see that even the Roman church, thousands of miles from Jerusalem, had embraced community. In Acts 28:15 Paul was encouraged by Roman Christians who "walked at least 33 miles from Rome to meet him—a sacrificial expression of kindness and warmth."[10] What a picture of a caring community!

Perhaps the strongest argument for the depth of community seen within the early church is that community didn't exist only when everything was new and exciting. This environmental element was strong in the midst of tough times and persecution. For example:

- Peter and John experienced support and love from fellow believers after being questioned by the Sanhedrin: "On their release, Peter and John went back to their own people and reported all that the chief priests and elders had said to them. When they heard this, they raised their voices together in prayer to God." (Acts 4:23-24a).
- In Acts 14, Paul was stoned, dragged out of the city, and left for dead. The disciples of Lystra "gathered around" Paul until he was strong enough to go "back into the city" (v. 20). Don't hurry through this passage; enter the experience. Paul was stoned and left for dead. Imagine his fear. Imagine the fear of these disciples. Yet in spite of the pain and fear, Paul courageously returned to the city. Part of his courage must have originated from this loving community. Later, Paul strengthened and encouraged these followers to remain true to the faith by saying, "We must go through many hardships to enter the kingdom of God" (v. 22). What a picture of authentic community in the midst of persecution!

CULTIVATE—JESUS CREATING A TRANSFORMATIONAL ENVIRONMENT

The community we see in the book of Acts found its start in the ministry of Jesus. Remember, from the beginning, Jesus knew this group of individual brokers would have to become a band of brothers that would lead the early church. This reality influenced how he led. This means the fully-developed Polaroid snapshot of community in the book of Acts had its origins in the Gospels. Jesus lived, taught, and modeled community so that once he was no longer on earth, his disciples would know how to cultivate community.

Specifically, notice how the community we see in the book of Acts has simple beginnings in the love and intentional relationship building of Jesus. First, Jesus modeled intentional relationships by becoming flesh and dwelling among us (John 1:14). There isn't a better example of intentionality than God becoming a human in order to be with us and make himself known. His public ministry was also about intentionality. For instance, he intentionally rubbed shoulders with people by going to them. In Mark 1:29-31, Jesus went to the home of his early followers; in John 1:43, Jesus found Philip; and in John 3:22, Jesus "spent some time with" his followers. The Greek word used in this last verse is *diatribo,* which means to "rub off on." Jesus intentionally built relationships in such a way as to "rub off on" his followers.

Having called his men, Jesus made a practice of being with them....When one stops to think of it, this was an incredibly simple way of doing it. Jesus had no formal school, no seminaries, no outlined course of study, no periodic membership classes in which he enrolled his followers. None of these highly organized procedures....As amazing as it may seem, all Jesus did to teach these men his ways was to draw them close to himself.

—Robert Coleman
The Master Plan of Evangelism

And what was rubbing off? Love.

Love is a powerful platform for authentic community, so Jesus made it foundational to his ministry. The following samples from the later portion of the book of John demonstrates just how Jesus' love rubbed off on his followers:

- "Now Jesus loved Martha and her sister and Lazarus" (John 11:5).
- "It was just before the Passover Festival. Jesus knew that the hour had come for him to leave this world and go to the Father. Having loved his own who were in the world, he loved them to the end" (John 13:1).
- "A new command I give you: Love one another. As I have loved you, so you must love one another" (John 13:34).
- "Whoever has my commands and keeps them is the one who loves me. Anyone who loves me will be loved by my Father, and I too will love them and show myself to them" (John 14:21).
- "As the Father has loved me, so have I loved you. Now remain in my love" (John 15:9).
- "My command is this: Love each other as I have loved you. Greater love has no one than this: to lay down one's life for one's friends" (John 15:12-13).
- "My prayer is....they may be brought to complete unity. Then the world will know that you sent me and have loved them even as you have loved me. Father, I want those you have given me to be with me where I am, and to see my glory, the glory you have given me because you loved me before the creation of the world.

Righteous Father, though the world does not know you, I know you, and they know that you have sent me. I have made you known to them, and will continue to make you known in order that the love you have for me may be in them and that I myself may be in them" (John 17:20a, 23b-26).

- "When they had finished eating, Jesus said to Simon Peter, 'Simon son of John, do you truly love me more than these?' 'Yes, Lord,' he said, 'you know that I love you.' Jesus said, 'Feed my lambs.' Again Jesus said, 'Simon son of John, do you love me?' He answered, 'Yes, Lord, you know that I love you.' Jesus said, 'Take care of my sheep.' The third time he said to him, 'Simon son of John, do you love me?' Peter was hurt because Jesus asked him the third time, 'Do you love me?' He said, 'Lord, you know all things; you know that I love you.' Jesus said, 'Feed my sheep'" (John 21:15-18a).

The love and intentionality of Jesus saturated his movement. His followers experienced his love in the flesh and saw him intentionally loving others (even the unlovely). Through these expressions, Christ cultivated authentic community among his followers; and his followers, in turn, cultivated the same environment within the early church.

YOUR TURN!

Just as Christ's vision of community was fleshed out as he rubbed shoulders with his followers, so too will your vision of authentic community be fleshed out as you rub shoulder with students. Remember, Jesus' daily actions cultivated true community. Over time, the right environmental rudiments gelled together and true community formed.

The next pages contain 25 ideas to help you cultivate community. But again remember, your job isn't to make community happen; true community happens only through the transformational work of Christ. Your job is to cultivate the right environment. So again, think of the following ideas as seeds to plant in your group's soil. Water the seeds, cultivate them, and you'll likely see God grow authentic community in your group.

And remember, the following ideas are starter seeds. Use them, but don't be overly dependent on them. If anything, let them cultivate better, deeper seeds for planting.

I value unity because I believe we learn truth from each other in this process.

- Rowan Williams -

26. BE A COMMUNITY METEOROLOGIST

One role youth workers play in cultivating environments for community is assessing the climate of their ministries. What is the relational temperature of your group? One way to find out is to ask. Give several trusted students and adult volunteers a list of atmospheric descriptions and let them circle the phrases they believe best describe the group. Their insights will be your community weather report.

27. DEFINE *COMMUNITY*

Have you ever noticed how youth workers use slang as a way to feel more hip? The cool terms in the '80s were *seeker-sensitive* and *church growth.* In the '90s it was *purpose-driven.* In the '00s it has been *postmodern* and *missional.* These words aren't bad, but many people use them badly. They throw them around without comprehending the depth of their meanings. I must confess, I've been guilty of this myself.

Community, if we're not careful, can be one of those words we use badly. I cringe when I hear youth workers using words such as *tribe* and *community* in inappropriate contexts. For example, I know of two college pastors who created a cult-like following. They spoke into anyone's life in practically any manner they wanted. If questioned, both would throw a yellow flag

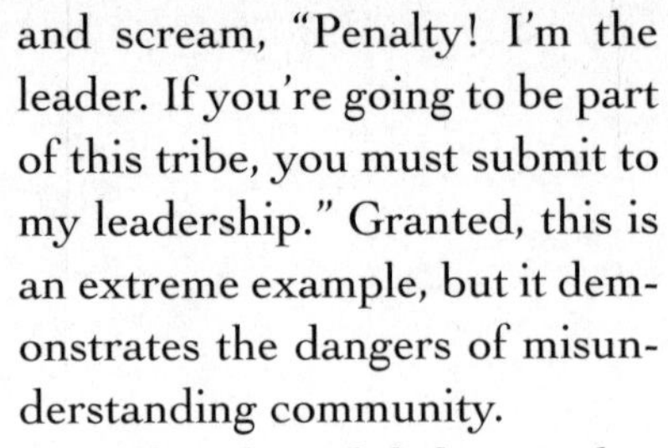

and scream, "Penalty! I'm the leader. If you're going to be part of this tribe, you must submit to my leadership." Granted, this is an extreme example, but it demonstrates the dangers of misunderstanding community.

The idea of defining what *community* actually means isn't too creative, but it's crucial. Wise youth workers regularly define and model true *fellowship, belonging, acceptance, unity,* and *community.* A good way to do this is to use the "one another" passages throughout the New Testament. And be sure your group understands the difference between just being a *tribe* and being a *tribe* committed to Christ.

28. IDENTITY

Does your group have an identity? Does it have a unique name, feel, vibe, and even logo? Or does your group go by a generic name such as *First Baptist Youth Group* or *The United Methodist High School Group?*

Having a positive identity is central to developing community; and while group names, logos, and T-shirts don't automatically create an identity, they sure can help. Additionally, the more unique and positive the name and identity, the better. Some of my favorite youth group names are *The Image, Overflow, Merge,* and *Core.* The students I've met in these ministries talk about their group with pride and are much more likely to invite friends.

In addition, having a cool name, logo, and T-shirts aren't magic pills. It's a sense of genuine community that makes students proud of their group; add a solid group name to authentic community, and you have a winning combo.

You also have a rallying point. Take the name *The Image.* This group uses the name as a major teaching theme. They want to be *the image* of Christ in their community, and they use their name as a constant reminder of why the group exists. It's their rallying cry that constantly centers their group.

So pick a name, design a logo, paint your youth group walls, and create T-shirts. But more than anything else, live the community message your name embodies.

29. WALLS OF REMEMBRANCE

Speaking of painting the walls, one of the quickest ways our ministry created a community feel was to plaster our walls with pictures of students. By no means did this lead to deeper fellowship, but it definitely cultivated a sense that our group was all about teenagers.

All we did was take photos from our most recent events, print out 8½ x 11 copies, place different colors of paper behind each one to create a frame, and slap them on the wall. Most students love seeing pictures of themselves, so when we plastered an entire wall with pictures from our most recent event, students gravitated to that wall during hangout time. As they looked at each photo, they were reminded of the great time they had during the event and started saying to each other, "Oh, this is when we did..." These pictures weren't merely good decorations, they were reminders to students that our group was about doing life together. This simple idea was so powerful that we made sure our "Wall of Remembrance" was constantly updated. We also made sure that the first night after every major event included a kickin' slide show with pictures of as many students as possible. These ideas proved powerful in creating a sense of belonging and excitement.

30. LOVE IS SPELLED T-I-M-E

Many new youth workers, especially volunteers, worry about what to say to students. "I don't know how to speak 'teenager,' and I'm afraid I'll say something stupid and look like an idiot."

Don't get too worked up about what to say because the time you devote speaks louder than your words. You simply cannot put a price tag on time. The act of being with students communicates volumes.

> *Be devoted to one another in love. Honor one another above yourselves.*
>
> —Romans 12:10

31. LOVE IS ALSO SPELLED T-U-R-F

If you really want to make good use of your T-I-M-E with students, spend it on their T-U-R-F. Show up at their schools, special events, and other important places. Obviously, you'll want to gauge the places according to your relationship. If you surprise a student you barely know by showing up unannounced at the school cafeteria...no points for you. But if you attend an event the student is involved in, such as a football game or a play, your actions communicate that you care about him. As the relationship grows deeper, a cafeteria lunch might move into the realm of realty and no longer seem too strange (even though the food will).

One last thought. Even if students don't seem to care if you show up (sorry, but it will happen), you're still making an impact. What other adults show up at their stuff? They might appear disinterested, but your presence won't go unnoticed.

32. TOP-10 LIST FOR CONTACTING STUDENTS

As long as we're on the subject of contacting (that's youth ministry lingo for spending time with students on their turf), here's a top-10 list for how to do it.

- **Number 10:** Learn names. No word sounds better to a teenager than his or her name.
- **Number 9:** Don't try to be one of the gang (sorry, you're not that cool). Teenagers don't need, or want, a balding buddy. They need and want an adult who cares enough to listen to them, talk with them, and model how to be a grown-up Christian.
- **Number 8:** NEVER make fun of them. Teenage humor can be ruthless, especially when it comes to pointing out their friends' flaws. Do NOT join in. You may think teasing breaks the ice, but you're only breaking their future trust in you.
- **Number 7:** Get to know other students through the relationships you already have. I've met hundreds of students by hanging out with teenagers I already know. This is the easiest and most natural way to expand your relationship network.
- **Number 6:** Pray for students you contact, as well as students you'd like to contact. Since it's God who transforms, go ahead and ask God to use your contacting efforts as a means of doing his work.
- **Number 5:** Ask questions. Questions show genuine interest.
- **Number 4:** Don't go too deep too quickly. If you're in the beginning stages of connecting with a student, don't ask

deeply personal questions; they'll come up naturally once a relationship is established. In the beginning, keep things light. Ask questions about school, activities, and friends.

- **Number 3:** Don't try too hard. I've seen adult leaders force their way into conversations with students. That's not building bridges; that's building barriers.
- **Number 2:** Don't talk too much about yourself, even if you were the starting quarterback of the state champion football team back in 1975. Sorry, but who cares? Not teenagers.
- **Number 1:** Be you! God made a youth worker just like you to connect with certain students in your group.

THINK ABOUT IT!

Wondering why contacting is in a community-building chapter? How does contacting build community in youth ministry?

Remember that two of the key components Jesus modeled for building an environment of community were intentional relationships and love. Contacting powerfully demonstrates both.

33. APPROPRIATE TOUCHES

If you've worked with teenagers for over a week, you've probably recognized how many are starved for affection. For these love-hungry kids, nothing champions Christ-like love like appropriate, physical displays of affection from genuine, caring adults. As Doug Fields says, "One of the ingredients for teenagers' emotional health is that they experience proper affection. Everyone has 'skin hunger,' and the hunger must be fed in appropriate ways. We must figure out how to touch kids in a safe manner that models Christ-like affection."[11]

However...

When it comes to physical touch, everyone has an opinion about what is and is not appropriate. Guy Wasko (a youth worker friend of mine) and I came up with a few thoughts that should help you formulate your own guidelines.[12]

TAKE NOTE...

There are no guarantees. Even if you set up what you believe is a full-proof system for keeping inappropriate touch from occurring, it can still happen. Humans are so creative when it comes to sin.

Your job, then, is to establish appropriate guidelines that church leaders support, communicate the guidelines clearly, and expect people to follow them. If someone breaks the guidelines, don't punish everyone by creating over-the-top rules. Deal with the individual while continuing to champion your well-thought-out plan with the rest of your team.

First, youth workers should establish written guidelines concerning what constitutes appropriate displays of affections for both student-to-student touch and adult-to-student touch. Don't go nuts and write a 25-page thesis; just make the guidelines clear and easy to understand. Also, get these guidelines approved by whatever church authority exists (governing board, elders, senior pastor, etc.) before presenting them to the youth group.

What makes this process difficult is that there's a fine line between protecting people from inappropriate behavior and becoming legalistic. Most would agree that handshakes, high fives, and the affirming pat on the back are fine; but what about other, more intimate touches? When addressing these more delicate matters, here are some questions to consider:

- What kind of hug is fitting? Are sideways, one-arm, shoulder hugs the only appropriate hug, or are frontal hugs okay?
- What is your PDA rule (Public Display of Affection)?

Second, once guidelines have been established, adult leaders must clearly and regularly communicate what appropriate, loving touches look like. This means volunteers must be trained in appropriate touch and encouraged to model this behavior. Keep communicating, training, and modeling, and soon everyone will know, almost instinctively, what is and isn't acceptable.

Third, a way to almost guarantee that only appropriate touch is occurring between leaders and students is to never allow adults to spend time alone with a student of the opposite sex (some even believe this guideline should be followed with adults and students of the same sex). Practically everyone who touches others in public does so in an appropriate manner, which means this approach automatically creates a high level of protection and accountability. If there are leaders who either demonstrate inappropriate expressions of affection publicly or break the "never alone" policy, be sure to immediately address your concerns with them individually and make sure they understand there is no leniency in this area.

> *As mature Christian leaders, we need to be able to model appropriate male/female affection. Obviously, we need to be careful here! Not only can inappropriate affection lead to inappropriate relationships, it can also send misleading and unintended messages to impressionable teenagers. I explain to my young leaders (those in their 20s) that there's a big difference between a student getting a hug from me (in my 40s, a father figure, married, my own kids in the youth group) and a hug from them.*
>
> **—Doug Fields**
> **"The Power of Affection"**
> ***Group Magazine* (Nov/Dec 2005)**

34. AT YOUR HOUSE—WORK IS FUN?

I'll never forget a father of a middle school student picking his son up from my house one afternoon. My small group had come over to help me do yard work and then watch a college football game with me. The dad was amazed that I could do a work day and have students show up. Reflectively he said, "At my house, yard work is work…at your house, it's fun."

There's a lot of truth to what this dad said. For some reason, especially with middle school students, what seems boring at their house is fun at my house (and according to most middle school students, everything is boring at their houses). Yard work, running errands, or just hanging out…the mundane isn't too mundane at the house of a youth worker.

Be sure you get the message: Everyday, ordinary activities are great opportunities to build intentional relationships with students.

TAKE NOTE...

The difference between small groups and "house groups" is, in many ways, an issue of semantics. However, in Acts 2:42-48, community seems to consist of more than three or four people getting together for prayer, study, and accountability. Hanging out in homes, eating together, and doing life together with a midsize group of believers seems like a more accurate picture of what was actually taking place.

35. NOT JUST SMALL GROUPS—HOUSE GROUPS

House groups were highlighted previously, but let's take a closer look to see how house groups build community. When a youth group reaches 30 or more, it enters the large group zone. As with the Twilight Zone, reality morphs into something unexpected in this case. Group members no longer know everyone, and the intimacy that was once part of your midsize community (i.e., a group of around 15 to 20 people) becomes much harder to reproduce.

So what's the solution? Most cheer: "Small groups! Small groups! Small groups!" But truth be told, these small group advocates are just trashing their vocal chords.

While most small group advocates see small groups as a way to build community, small groups actually do a better job creating space for in-depth teaching and accountability. Don't misunderstand: Accountability and in-depth teaching are good things and definitely ingredients of community; however, they represent the more intense ingredients of community. True community also involves more casual, social ingredients such as eating together, hospitality, hanging out with each other, and going to events together. These ingredients could be called "doing life together," and the best model for this is probably the midsize group.

So why not create space that allows for both intense and casual ingredients? Why not take two or three small groups, have them meet regularly in a home, encourage them to do life together, and *viola*...you have a *house group.*

When I first suggested house groups to volunteers, I heard groans. "Kent, I can't add another night to my weekly calendar; it's already packed." Yet that's one of the beauties of house groups—nights are *not* added.

For instance, if you have 30 or more students, set up two house groups (each made up of two or three small groups). Keep the small groups gender specific (e.g., girls' small groups and guys' small groups), but combine one or two girls' small groups with one or two guys' small groups to create a house group and have these groups meet in the same house weekly. This is multitasking at its best—several small accountability groups joining together to make one midsize community group...and both gatherings happen simultaneously.

What's killer about house groups is the variety they create. For instance, one week everyone in the house group can meet together for activities, announcements, and teaching, then small groups can break into different rooms for discussion and prayer. The next week all teaching can be done through small groups, and the house group time can be for prayer, connecting, and hanging out. I've even allowed students to teach the entire house group. Or when I find a student who's a good small group facilitator, I let her lead a small group all year. The options of what to do and how to do it are limitless when combining small groups into one house group.

THINK ABOUT IT...

I like having guys' small groups and girls' small groups form a house group. This way, as the youth ministry grows larger, students can still be connected with a midsize community of 15 to 20 guys and girls, but also go deep with a few individuals in their small group. In other words, this allows a large youth ministry to have several regular-sized youth groups within the context of their larger group.

A final word: Remember, house groups work best when time is not too limited. For instance, small accountability groups function well within the framework of an hour, but this won't work with House Groups. To accomplish small group accountability and midsize community in the same evening, two or three hours are required. House groups I've led usually look something like this:

- Eat a casual dinner together and catch up with each other
- Spend time as a house group engaged in a lesson, going over upcoming events, playing a game, or just hanging out
- Break into small groups for teaching, discussion, accountability, or prayer
- Get back together as a house group for a few minutes of prayer or just hanging out

36. SIX ACCOUNTABILITY TIPS FOR SMALL GROUPS

Accountability, especially for teenagers who want to grow in their commitments to Christ, is vital to cultivating authentic community. The best and most natural place to do this is within small groups, especially if you embrace the small group/house group ideas. During house group time, non-accountability ingredients such as hanging out, eating together, teaching, discussion, and even prayer can be championed. This frees up small groups to zero in on the deeper ingredients of community—interaction, application of teaching, prayer, and accountability.

Here are six tips for cultivating an accountability environment within small groups:

- **Tip 1: Keep small groups gender-based.** As a rule, same-sex groups work best for accountability.
- **Tip 2: Cultivate trust.** Remind students at the start of every meeting: "What's said here, stays here." This helps cultivate an environment of trust and support. If you discover a student breaking confidence, confront him immediately and be sure he knows his continued involvement depends upon confidentiality. And by all means, don't break confidence yourself.
- **Tip 3: Know when to make exceptions to confidence.** There are a few exceptions to the confidentiality rule. For instance, if someone's life is in danger, if the church has certain guidelines for when confidence should be broken, or if there's a legal obligation to tell someone else, then confidence must be broken. How do you do this? I've always told students, "I promise to keep everything confidential that I'm allowed to keep confidential. However, if you tell me something that I'm

responsible to tell someone else about, I will do so. Remember, however, I always have your very best interests at heart. I will only tell someone else when I know it is best for you; and I will only tell the person or persons that are supposed to know. You can trust me to do what's right."

- **Tip 4: Be vulnerable first.** Share personal victories and defeats. Without vulnerability, accountability doesn't happen. This means you must take the lead by being vulnerable first.
- **Tip 5: Be honest first.** Just as with vulnerability, accountability doesn't happen without honesty.
- **Tip 6: Ask good questions.** Accountability is enhanced when real-life questions are asked and answered. Consider asking these types of questions:
    - What are you doing in your time connecting with God?
    - How are you investing in the lives of others (those within the youth group and your non-churched friends)?
    - Do you have any strategies for how to best cultivate the important areas of your life (family relationships, school, job, friendships)?
    - What steps are you taking to make sure you're above reproach in relationships, especially in dating relationships?
    - Are there any sins you're flirting with, such as lust, gossip, lying, immorality, etc.?
    - How can we best pray for and support you?

37. OPEN CLIQUES

Do you have a favorite superhero? You know...Batman? Superman? Underdog?

One of mine is Superman. Faster than a speeding bullet! More powerful than a locomotive! Able to leap tall building in a single bound! Add X-ray vision and being secure enough to wear tights (not to mention red underwear outside his tights), and you have yourself a superhero.

Yet even Superman has a weakness (besides the red underwear and tights). Kryptonite. If exposed to this green stuff, Superman becomes weak.

Have you ever noticed, though, that when Superman encounters kryptonite, he still wins? I even recall a number of episodes where he used kryptonite, the very thing his nemesis employed to destroy him, as a means to defeat his enemy. Amazing!

There's one weakness every youth ministry faces regardless of its size or stature: Cliques. Like kryptonite, cliques wreak havoc in otherwise heroic ministries. What's more, Satan, our nemesis, uses cliques to destroy the authentic community we try so hard to cultivate. But like Superman, we can turn Satan's kryptonite against him. How? By opening the doors to closed cliques.

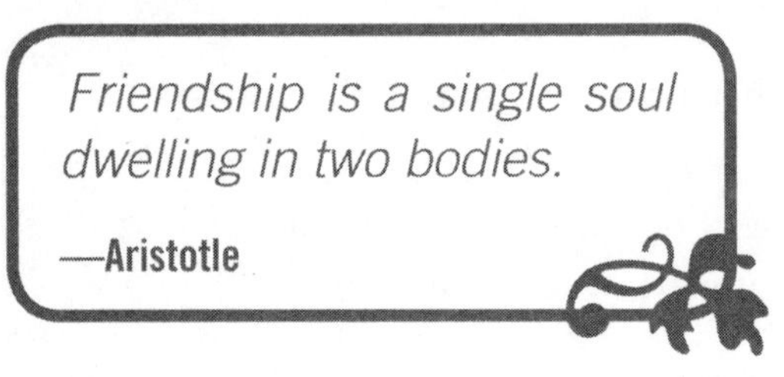

Friendship is a single soul dwelling in two bodies.

—Aristotle

Most cliques are *closed* groupings of students who become so connected with each other that outsiders find breaking into Fort Knox easier. These unofficial groupings have community, but of a clogged nature.

Open cliques are very different. Students in these groupings, while connected with each other, don't deadbolt others out. They appreciate their smaller, tight-knit community of friends, but they also engage with the larger community of the youth ministry. These cliques enhance, rather than hinder, true community.

By no means are open cliques natural, but neither are they impossible to foster. Here are some tips that should help unlock the doors of most closed cliques.

- **Encourage friendship grouping.** Often we advertise youth group as a great place for teenagers to build friendships, only to get upset when they actually connect with a small group of friends. Don't discourage friendship groupings; encourage them.

- **Teach, at least annually, on biblical community** and be sure to explain the difference between open and closed cliques.

- **Regularly remind students of the difference between open and closed cliques.** Since friendship groups naturally close over time, it's not uncommon to see cliques close up. Therefore, regularly remind students of the youth ministry's commitment to open cliques. Keep applauding friendship groupings, but consistently encourage groups to open up.

- **Hold ministry-level students accountable.** One of the greatest skills ministry-level students can develop is friendship building. Therefore, equip and hold them accountable for reaching out to others. At the same time, be careful not to crush them. Even ministry-level students can feel like Lone Rangers when it comes to building friendships with strangers. Remind them that they have groups of friends in the youth group with whom visitors can hang out. Remember, the goal is open groups, not just open individuals.
- **Use house groups as natural ways to build open cliques.** Be sure house group leaders understand that the best place to model true friendships with a few people, yet still be open to others, is in house groups.

38. WHEELS

What is it about "wheels" that cultivate community? Rollerblading in a park, going to an "old school" skating rink, biking, going on van rides to a retreat center, or just running errands with students in the car…for some reason, these activities create connections. So here's an idea that's as practical as it gets: Train all adult volunteers to use one "wheels" opportunity each month to contact students. If you have five adult volunteers, that's a potential for five intentional relationship-building opportunities a month. This equals 60 in one year! These simple 60 "wheels" experiences will go a long way toward cultivating an environment of community within your group.

39. THE FOOD NETWORK

Cooking is all the rage. With shows such as *30-Minute Meals with Rachael Ray* and *Ace of Cakes,* cooking shows have a late-night variety feel to them. What's more, these shows aren't just for girls; programs such as *Guy's Big Bite* and *BBQ with Bobby Flay* especially demonstrate that.

How do cooking shows relate to community in youth ministry?

If you've been around church for more than say, two seconds, you know nothing builds community like eating. Jesus ate with his disciples. The early church ate together regularly. In fact, eating has become such a part of today's church culture that the word *fellowship* is practically synonymous with potlucks, church basements, and linoleum. So these cooking shows can be tools for building on the church tradition of eating together and a way of moving fellowship to the 21st century.

So to all the women reading this sentence, the next time you have a sleepover with your small group, make it a cooking night. Light candles. Play music. Pour glasses of sparkling grape juice. Then prepare an awesome dinner together.

Guys, next time you host a Super Bowl Party or watch the Final Four with a group of guys, don't just order pizza and wings...prepare them yourself.

Want to really use this approach to your advantage? Then don't just cook for special events, make it a regular occurrence. For instance, if your ministry has house groups, have groups cook a meal together monthly. My wife plans cooking nights for our house groups, and I'm continually amazed at how our community "feel" increases each time we're all in the kitchen together.

40. SHORT FILMS

Do you have artsy students and creative adult volunteers? Then hook them up to create short films together. This accomplishes two things: First, community develops among this team. Second, you'll end up with some unique teaching resources.

As a side note, Larry, the volunteer who oversaw our Creative Arts team in one church at which I served, was a community genius. His team was made up of students who did drama, A/V, music, and dance, and most of them were big-time committed, not just to the Creative Arts team but also to the ministry at large. This commitment started at the top, though: Larry championed a high level of ownership to the ministry himself, and his commitment trickled down through the Creative Arts team.

41. VIDEO YEARBOOKS

Speaking of short films, why not get your Creative Arts team to annually develop a video yearbook? This was a highlight in our middle school group. We sold them at cost and always sold out. What's more, I've had students in high school, college, and even young professionals come up to me and say things such as, "Kent, I watched the video yearbook from my middle school years last night, and I laughed and cried through the whole thing. Those were such good times, and it reminded me how much I grew in my walk with Christ during those years." Seriously, this happens all the time.

Here are two other suggestions: With high school, make it a senior video instead of a video yearbook. I've found that video yearbooks sell like crazy in middle school, but not so much in high school. But every senior wants to buy a senior video! What's more, we showed it during our senior banquet, which most of our underclassmen attended. So it created memories for all our students and gave underclassmen something to anticipate during their senior year.

Another idea: Do major event videos. We always produced a *Mission Mexico* video, and students purchased these in droves. Our goal wasn't to make money, but to capture memories. These videos helped create a sense of belonging and significance. I've regularly had grown adults tell me, "I watched the *Mission Mexico* video last night. What a trip...it changed my life! I'm so glad I was part of our youth group!"

42. PROPER CHALLENGES

Do you have a systematic approach to challenging students to step it up? Many youth workers complain about lack of leadership among students, yet they have no strategy for challenging or championing student leadership. Why not use strategic moments to help students step to the plate?

In our middle school ministry, we used an end-of-the-year trip not only to say goodbye to graduating eighth-graders, but also to challenge outgoing seventh graders to step it up. We even created a program that gave key graduating eighth-grade students a chance to tell the seventh-graders why they loved our group so much, and how they could be leaders in our group. It was a powerful event. Additionally, we followed it up during the summer months with an event called "Take a Step Retreat." Through challenge courses and a ropes course, we stretched our new potential leaders physically, mentally, and spiritually. We encouraged them by telling them the difference between a good year and a great year in our group was the quality of our eighth-grade leadership. We challenged them to own the destiny of our youth group.

In high school, we used the senior banquet as a chance to challenge new leaders. We asked key seniors to reflect on what our group meant to them during their high school years and to challenge key students to step up to the plate in the coming years. We also had a few key summer experiences that helped new high school leaders step up to the plate.

You don't have to do any of the things described here, but you do need a plan. How will you strategically challenge students to step it up and help you cultivate community?

Listening moves us closer, it helps us become more whole, more healthy, more holy. Not listening creates fragmentation, and fragmentation is the root of all suffering.

—Margaret J. Wheatley

43. DON'T JUST LISTEN... HEAR

One of Stephen Covey's seven habits of highly effective people is: *Seek first to understand, then to be understood.* The key to understanding someone, of course, is listening. Not just listening, but listening actively so you genuinely hear what's being said. If every adult leader would develop active listening skills, community would be almost guaranteed.

Here are six effective active listening qualities that will help you listen *and* hear:

- Be genuinely interested in teenagers and their stories.
- Look people in the eyes.
- Realize you don't have all the right answers.
- Acknowledge emotions and feelings.
- Display a nonjudgmental attitude.
- Follow up with people after a conversation.

Remember, good listeners are actively engaged in conversations. This takes practice. But the more you practice, the more your attitude will say to teenagers, "I really care about you."

44. A DOZEN FRIENDSHIP SKILLS TO MODEL

Friendships are at the core of community. What's more, *good* friendships provide support, encouragement, accountability, joy, strength, and more.

How can you cultivate an environment within your youth ministry that fosters the development of good friendships? One way is to model authentic friendships in your own life and with students. Here are 12 skills to consider when developing good friends:

1. **Communicate.** Good communication is foundational to good friendships. Model good communication by listening well and authentically sharing thoughts and feelings.
2. **Listen.** Even though listening is part of good communication, it desires a spot of its own. It's that important. As I've heard Jim Burns say numerous times, "Listening is the language of love."
3. **Be positive.** "Leading behavioral researchers have told us that as much as *77 percent* of everything we think about is negative, counterproductive, and works against us."[13] Such negative programming, in many cases, is unintentional. It comes from teachers, parents, siblings, peers, and the media. But negative input, even if unintentional, is still negative. If you want to develop *good* friendships, be positive—and especially look for the positive in obviously negative situations. I don't know about you, but these are the kind of people I want to befriend.
4. **Don't gossip.** "The perverse stir up dissension, and gossips separate close friends" (Proverbs 16:28). Enough said.
5. **Fight fair.** Friends fight. Not smack-downs, but they disagree and argue. One way you can tell if a friendship is mature is if friends disagree agreeably.
6. **Sacrifice.** Whether you agree with popular self-help guru Wayne Dyer or not, he's definitely right about one thing: "It's never crowded along the extra mile." True friends travel the extra mile for each other.
7. **Be there.** Friends are available for each other, especially when the going gets tough.
8. **Invest time.** Time is the greatest investment a person can make in a friendship.
9. **Love.** Love "always protects, always trusts, always hopes, always perseveres" (1 Corinthians 13:7).

10. **Tell the truth.** Dishonesty destroys friendships. Good friends tell the truth, even if it's painful.
11. **Let go.** True friends forgive mistakes, hurts, and wrongdoings. Good friends know how to let go and move on.
12. **Be loyal.** Loyalty is a key ingredient of real friendships.

45. SMALL GROUP CONTACTING NIGHTS

One of the best things we ever did for our middle school ministry was schedule "contacting" into our small group calendar. Here's how it worked.

Our small groups met on Sunday nights at the church and followed a five-week-on, one-week-off schedule. For years, all five nights revolved around what many would consider typical small group meetings—Bible study, accountability, and prayer. One year we decided to make small groups more holistic, and one way we did this was to change our schedule. Our five evenings now followed a schedule similar to this:

Night 1: Contact Night

Nights 2, 3, and 4: Small Groups

Night 5: Corporate Worship or Service Project

That first night—the contacting night—revolutionized our ministry. We gave the entire night to relationship building. Adult leaders could take their small group students anywhere and do anything. The only exceptions were movies and video games. These were off limits because they didn't promote interaction; but practically every other teenager-friendly activity was fair game. We had groups playing ultimate Frisbee, getting dressed up to go out to fancy dinners, playing board games, bowling, rollerblading, hosting their own scavenger hunt, and more.

This strategy proved to be revolutionary for a number of reasons. First, it guaranteed our volunteers were contacting students. Until then, contacting for many volunteers was hit and miss. This approach guaranteed students were in relational settings with their leaders at least six or seven times during a school year.

Second, the depth of relationships built between adults and students grew much deeper much faster. Generally speaking, within a few months relationships were much deeper than in years past. Why? Because adults were strategically investing time and energy into relationships.

Third, even though we were giving up a teaching night during every series, lessons were more readily received by students because relationships were deeper. What's more, adult leaders had more real-life teaching opportunities with students because they were hanging out with students more.

This schedule became tradition after just one year. It was perhaps the best move we ever made with our small group ministry, and it's one that'll work well with high school students also.

(Note: The new middle school pastor at this church has taken this concept even further; his idea is explained in the Truth-and-Grace Ideas coming up next.)

46. NET-WORK

In today's world, community can be built even when your group isn't meeting. How? Through the magic of the Internet! Web sites, emails, blogs, instant messaging, MySpace and Facebook—and by the time this book is published, probably a couple of other great tools. Do you need to be vigilant in how your group uses the Internet? Yes. But don't let fear or lack of know-how keep you from tapping into these great tools.

47. OPEN HOUSE

One of my heroes is Dan Glaze, a volunteer youth worker who led the youth group in my church when I was in high school. Dan impacted my life like no other person, but it wasn't his teaching or the events he planned that cultivated an environment for transformation in my life. It was his house. Dan was incredibly hospitable and regularly opened the doors of his house—and it was there our tiny youth group gelled and grew together.

Want to cultivate community in your group? Open your house.

48. COMMUNITY RETREAT

Many youth groups host winter or spring retreats, usually for one or two reasons. First, and probably most importantly, they use their retreats as means of outreach. Second, they use their retreats to tap into the momentum that's been created so far during the year. Stronger momentum usually means stronger attendance at a retreat.

Here's a different approach to consider: How about hosting a fall retreat for the *opposite* reasons? First, don't use a fall retreat for outreach; use it to cultivate community. About six weeks after school starts, plan an amazingly fun, interactive weekend and make it a highlight of the year. In the midst of all the fun, intentionally discuss authentic community. Explain, illustrate, and practice how to build community.

> *Friendship is...not something you learn in school. But if you haven't learned the meaning of friendship, you really haven't learned anything.*
>
> —Muhammad Ali

Second, instead of waiting for momentum, use this retreat to create it. Think about it—one 48-hour weekend equals the same amount of time as an entire year of small group meetings.

49. CIRCLES OF CONCERN

Circles of Concern were highlighted previously as a means of helping ministry-level students pray for peers, but this tool can be used for so much more. As a reminder, Circles of Concern is a focusing tool. Students list six friends on whom to focus: three friends who don't have relationships with Christ and three students within the youth group. Students are instructed to pray deeply about whom they believe God wants on their lists, and once their lists are compiled, the people on the list become their prayer focus.

But this list can be more than a prayer focus. It can also be a *ministry* focus. Train students in relationship-building skills, then encourage them to make the people on their lists their relational priorities. Even if you only did this with your ministry team students, the community impact within your group could be outstanding. For instance, if your group has 30 regular attendees and five are ministry-level students, this means half the students within your group will receive relational focus from ministry-level students, as well as 15 non-Christian students within your town.

50. FROM COMMUNITY 101 TO 401

Cultivating an environment of community takes time. But as I note previously, time isn't the only issue. The intensity of each experience plays a role as well. For instance, encouraging students to create Open Cliques is much less intense than holding them accountable with their Circles of Concern. What's more, as an atmosphere of community develops, you'll have students at all ends of the community spectrum. This again means the best suggestion I can make for moving both your ministry and individuals from Community 101 to Community 401 is to take a multilevel approach. Here are some thoughts:

Outreach-level opportunities. Outreach experiences don't have to be filled with bells and whistles. Genuine community is a powerful outreach tool, and in many cases, even more powerful than any entertainment we can think up. Look for chances to allow non-churched students to connect with your group in natural, everyday ways.

Growth-level opportunities. Community must be a key component of all growth-level programming. Remember, growth almost always occurs within the context of relationships. Your teaching ministry can be incredible, yet transformation will be unlikely unless authentic community is cultivated. Therefore, just as much time and energy should be given to cultivating community as to teaching, praying, or worship.

Ministry-level opportunities. Empower ministry-level students to cultivate community. Train them to build genuine friendships, use Circles of Concern, and hold them accountable for opening up their cliques to others.

BONUS IDEAS: SUGGESTED RESOURCES

You know by now that the ideas in this book are designed to jump-start your brain. Want to go deeper? Check out some of these great resources:

- *A Tribe Apart* by Patricia Hersch
- *Hurt* by Chap Clark
- *Community-Building Ideas for Ministry with Young Teens* by Marilyn Kielbasa
- *Ideas Library* CD-ROM by Youth Specialties
- *Girls Ministry 101* by Whitney Prosperi (packed with specific community building ideas for girls)
- *Friendzee: Close Connections Edition* Game by Group Publishing
- *Building Community in Youth Groups* by Denny Rydberg
- *Youth Group Trust Builders* by Denny Rydberg

PREFACE TO PART 3

For the law was given through Moses;
grace and truth came through Jesus Christ.

- The Apostle John -

Truth-and-Grace. The purpose for cultivating an environment of truth-and-grace in youth ministry is to create a setting in which God's Word is central to belief and behavior. In such an atmosphere, God's Word becomes the standard, the basis of everything taught and valued. Even more it becomes the benchmark for obedience, and the measure by which all of life is assessed. The focus of an environment of truth and grace is *downward* from God—God revealing grace and truth to his people.

From the start Jesus' disciples seemed hungry for divine truth, so hungry that many were willing to leave everything and follow him. Over time this hunger grew, so much so that when Jesus asked his closest followers if they would leave with the crowd, Peter replied, "To whom shall we go? You have the words of eternal life" (John 6:68). How did Jesus cultivate such a strong desire for raw truth in his followers?

CLICK—JESUS BEGAN WITH THE END IN MIND

Again, let's begin by getting a clear picture of Jesus' fulfilled vision of truth and grace—a picture from the book of Acts. In Acts 2:42-47 we see the early church's commitment to God's truth and grace fleshed out through their devotion to the apostles' teaching, meeting together in the temple courts, and their regular observance of the Lord's Supper. Each was an *expression* of their allegiance to Christ's truth and grace.

Other examples abound in the book of Acts:

- In Acts 4, the priest and Sadducees "were greatly disturbed because the apostles were teaching the people, proclaiming in Jesus the resurrection of the dead. They seized Peter and John... put them in jail....But many who heard the message believed; so the number of men who believed grew to about five thousand" (vv. 2-4). When questioned the next day by the rulers, elders, and teachers, along with Annas the high priest, Caiaphas, John, Alexander, and the other men of the high priest's family (v. 6), Peter broke into a passionate exposition of the truth that Jesus is the Messiah. "When they saw the courage of Peter and John and realized that they were unschooled, ordinary men, they were astonished and they took note that these men had been with Jesus" (v. 13). After further discussion amongst themselves, the religious leaders called Peter and John in once again and "commanded them not to speak or teach at all in the name of Jesus. But Peter and John replied, 'Which is right in God's eyes: to listen to you, or to him? You be the judges! As for us, we cannot help speaking about what we have seen and heard'" (vv. 18-20).
- In Acts 5, the apostles' commitment to the truth stirred up trouble again. And once again, they appeared "before the Sanhedrin to be questioned by the high priest. 'We gave you strict orders not to teach in this name,' he said. 'Yet you have filled Jerusalem with your teaching and are determined to make us guilty of this man's blood.' Peter and the other apostles replied: 'We must obey God rather than human beings!''' (vv. 27-29).
- "Day after day, in the temple courts and from house to house, they never stopped teaching and proclaiming the good news that Jesus is the Messiah" (Acts 5:42).
- "After they had further proclaimed the word of the Lord and testified about Jesus, Peter and John returned to Jerusalem, preaching the gospel in many Samaritan villages" (Acts 8:25).
- When the proconsul of Paphos saw Paul deal with Elymas the sorcerer, "He believed, for he was amazed at the teaching about the Lord" (Acts 13:12)
- In Thessalonica, "as was his custom, Paul went into the synagogue, and on three Sabbath days he reasoned with them from the Scriptures, explaining and proving that the Messiah had to suffer and rise from the dead. 'This Jesus I am proclaiming to you is the Messiah,' he said. Some of the Jews were persuaded

and joined Paul and Silas, as did a large number of God-fearing Greeks and not a few prominent women" (Acts 17:2-4).

- In Athens, Paul "stood up in the meeting of the Areopagus and said: 'People of Athens! I see that in every way you are very religious. For as I walked around and looked carefully at your objects of worship, I even found an altar with this inscription: TO AN UNKNOWN GOD. So you are ignorant of the very thing you worship—and this is what I am going to proclaim to you" (Acts 17:22-23). He went on to declare the truth of Jesus.
- In spite of dire difficulty in the city of Corinth, Paul was prompted by God to stay put. "So Paul stayed in Corinth for a year and a half, teaching them the word of God" (Acts 18:11).
- Paul declared boldly to the Ephesian elders, "For I have not hesitated to proclaim to you the whole will of God" (Acts 20:27).

The strongest argument for the depth of the early church's commitment to truth and grace is not that they were committed when everything was new and exhilarating. Their commitment seems strongest in the midst of the harshest moments. This rugged commitment reveals that truth had become an environmental ingredient embedded within the DNA of the early church.

Before moving on, one other insight about an environment of truth needs mentioning. You've probably noticed I often speak of an environment of truth by using the phrase "truth and grace" (or "grace

THINK ABOUT IT...

John 1:17 is not a rejection of Moses and the law, and it's not saying that "grace" was not available within the law. The contrast here isn't the law against grace and truth because both come from the same gracious God. Rather the contrast is between the verbs was given *and* came. *God's grace* was given *through the law, but it* came *through Christ (i.e., the Word* became *flesh). The difference is one of degree and personalization. Grace and truth* coming *through Jesus is a more complete, personal reality. In fact, Christ added upon the grace that was already given through the law.*

and truth"). The reason is that cultivating this environment requires commitment to embracing both grace and truth. One without the other creates dysfunction. Let me explain...

In John 1:17 we are told: "For the law was given through Moses; grace and truth came through Jesus Christ." Throughout the Gospels, we see Jesus' life and message proclaiming God's truth and grace. In fact, he never shied away from proclaiming truth because the core message of truth is all about God's grace.

The early church followed his lead here as well. Notice how grace is central to their teaching of truth:

- "With great power the apostles continued to testify to the resurrection of the Lord Jesus. And God's grace was so powerfully at work in them all" (Acts 4:33).
- "When he [Barnabas] arrived and saw what the grace of God had done, he was glad and encouraged them all to remain true to the Lord with all their hearts" (Acts 11:23).
- "When the congregation was dismissed, many of the Jews and devout converts to Judaism followed Paul and Barnabas, who talked with them and urged them to continue in the grace of God" (Acts 13:43).
- "So Paul and Barnabas spent considerable time there, speaking boldly for the Lord, who confirmed the message of his grace by enabling them to perform signs and wonders" (Acts 14:3).
- "When Apollos wanted to go to Achaia, the believers encouraged him and wrote to the disciples there to welcome him. When he arrived, he was a great help to those who by grace had believed. For he vigorously refuted the Jews in public debate, proving from the Scriptures that Jesus was the Messiah" (Acts 18:27-28).
- In Paul's farewell to the church in Ephesus: "Now I commit you to God and to the word of his grace, which can build you up and give you an inheritance among all those who are sanctified" (Acts 20:32).

Throughout Christian history, grace and truth have gotten out of balance, and the church has often used both of its hands to clinch one or the other. Of course, overemphasizing one while deemphasizing the other leads to dysfunction. Think about it:

- When believers overemphasize grace and deemphasize truth, they become liars. Why? Because without truth, grace is no longer grace; it's just a feel-good wimpiness that refuses to address hard issues. It's powerless.

- When believers overemphasize truth and deemphasize grace, they become abusive. Why? Because without grace, truth is no longer truth; it's just the hard facts about our total depravity and God's perfect righteousness—and both become a giant club to browbeat people.

It seems as though the early church, however, knew how to hold onto both. It wasn't perfect, but the evidence is clear that truth and grace were championed equally. How did the early church know how to do this? Jesus passed it on to them. Therefore, since grace and truth *came through* Jesus, let's take a closer look at how he cultivated this environment within his earthly ministry.

CULTIVATE—JESUS CREATING A TRANSFORMATIONAL ENVIRONMENT

The environment of truth and grace seen in the book of Acts finds its start in the ministry of Jesus. Remember, from the beginning Jesus knew his followers would lead the early church in the truth and grace of God. This reality influenced how Jesus led. This means the pictures of truth and grace seen in the book of Acts have their origins in the Gospels. Jesus lived, taught, and modeled truth and grace so that once he was no longer on earth, his disciples knew how to cultivate the same.

How is the early church's commitment to truth and grace seen in the patterns of Christ's ministry? For one, God's Word was central to everything Jesus taught and how he lived. Jesus knew the Word, and it was central in his encounters. The New Testament records that Jesus "referred to the Old Testament more than eighty times, quoting from over seventy different chapters."[14] We see Jesus using the Word in warfare against Satan, to communicate his Father's heart, and to combat the Pharisees.

Even more, Jesus used Scripture to show he was the Messiah, for he knew that only when people understood who he was, and why he came would they truly follow him. That's why Jesus not only taught Scripture but also claimed that his words were as authoritative and truthful as Scripture. He wanted people to know that both the Scriptures and he himself were the Word of God. This is why:

- The apostle John claims: "The Word became flesh and made his dwelling among us. We have seen his glory, the glory of the one and only [Son], who came from the Father, full of grace and truth" (John 1:14).

- Jesus said he was the fulfillment of Scripture: "Do not think that I have come to abolish the Law or the Prophets; I have not come to abolish them but to fulfill them" (Matthew 5:17).
- Jesus used the Scripture to testify about himself: "You study the Scriptures diligently because you think that in them you possess eternal life. These are the very Scriptures that testify about me, yet you refuse to come to me to have life" (John 5:39-40).
- Jesus used the Word to show his followers that he was the Messiah: "And beginning with Moses and all the Prophets, he explained to them what was said in all the Scriptures concerning himself" (Luke 24:27).

In fact, notice the progression below from the book of John. Jesus talks about God's transforming truth, then claims his teaching is God's transforming truth, and finally boldly proclaims he's God's transforming truth:

- "But those who live by the truth come into the light, so that it may be seen plainly that what they have done has been done in the sight of God" (John 3:21).
- "If you hold to my teaching, you are really my disciples. Then you will know the truth, and the truth will set you free" (John 8:31b-32).
- "I am the way and the truth and the life. No one comes to the Father except through me" (John 14:6).

Many other examples could be given of how Jesus cultivated an environment of truth within his ministry. But he didn't use truth as a club. He spoke the truth boldly, yet graciously. Why? Because his message of truth was fundamentally the message of God's grace.

YOUR TURN!

In today's youth culture, there's much confusion regarding who Jesus is. To some teenagers, he's a cuss word. To most, he's just a nice guy such as Mr. Roarke of *Fantasy Island*—a character dressed in white who can't be known personally, but whose main purpose is to make your dreams come true. Yet knowing the truth about who Jesus is, what he's done for us, and who we can be in him is foundational to transformation.

This means youth ministries, instead of talking about God's Word, must cultivate an environment that gets students into God's Word. Even more, when in the Word, we must make a beeline to Christ. As Rick Lawrence, executive editor of *Group Magazine*, says, "It's time to get radical: Never again teach from the Bible, or plan a Bible study, or do a topical study, without making a beeline to Jesus."[15]

This is something eminent preacher Charles Spurgeon did. When a young man said to Spurgeon, "We are not to be preaching Christ always; we must preach what is in the text," Spurgeon responded, "Don't you know, young man, that from every town, and every village, and every little hamlet in England, wherever it may be, is a road to London?" "Yes," said the young man. "Ah!" said the old preacher, "and so from every text in Scripture is a road to the metropolis of Scriptures—that is Christ. Dear brother, when you get to a biblical text, say, 'Now, what is the road to Christ?' and then preach a sermon, running along the road toward the great metropolis—Christ."[16]

It's time to make the truth and grace of Christ central to youth ministry again. Not games, not concerts, not social science, not hot topics—Christ.

In the next pages are 25 ideas that will help you make a beeline to Christ. But once again, let me remind you that our job is not to make students accept truth. This comes only through the transformational work of God. Our job is to cultivate environments of grace and truth.

THINK ABOUT IT...

Even though church attendance is up for U.S. teenagers, according to the National Study of Youth and Religion, approximately 90 percent don't have a "committed" or "devoted faith." This means:

- *Faith in Christ isn't a central feature of their lives.*
- *Knowledge of the Christian faith is not even at a basic level.*
- *They have no clue as to how Christ can impact everyday lives.*

Religion seems very much a part of the lives of many U.S. teenagers, but for most of them it is in ways that seem quite unfocused, implicit, in the background, just part of the furniture.

—Christian Smith
Soul Searching

I believe that unarmed truth and unconditional love will have the final word in reality.

- Martin Luther King, Jr.

51. BALANCE YOUR FOCUS

The first two tips are short and sweet, but perhaps more important than any other. First, balance your teaching focus between *truth* and *grace*. The problem, of course, is that we all tend to emphasize one over the other.

When grace is prioritized over truth, a ministry becomes flaky and laissez-faire. Communicating Christ's unconditional love for students is a very good thing, but leaving out the fact that this unconditional love requires a response from us means we're selling a half-truth (which is a polite way of saying we're lying). Truly loving Christ, according to Jesus himself, requires obedience (John 14:23-24). This means when talking about loving Christ with all our hearts, we must tie it to obedience. To do otherwise means we're not teaching the whole counsel of God.

> *With great power the apostles continued to testify to the resurrection of the Lord Jesus. And God's grace was so powerfully at work in them all.*
>
> **—Acts 4:33**

On the flip side, truth without grace is abusive. I've met youth workers who like to lay out the "hard, cold facts of truth," and then tell students to "take it or leave it." Sorry, but such a detached, authoritarian approach leads to hard, cold

legalism. And legalism is more concerned with following the rules than with following Christ.

The right balance between truth and grace is summed up well in a statement I heard Dr. Steve Brown of Key Life Network attribute to the late Jack Miller: "Cheer up, you are so much worse than you think you are. But cheer up, God's grace is infinitely better than you can imagine."

52. BALANCE YOUR APPROACH

Although Jesus spent lots of time teaching the crowds, he spent significantly more time teaching his disciples. One of the likely reasons for this approach is that he wanted his followers to realize his teaching wasn't about facts alone, but about follow-through. This leads to the second short-but-sweet tip. According to Jesus, there needs to be a balance between *hearing* and *obeying*.

> *Every word of God proves true. He is a shield to all who come to him for protection.*
>
> **—Proverbs 30:5 (NLT)**

What this means to youth workers is that in our approach to teaching, we need to determine the best ways to balance teaching facts and providing opportunities for follow-through. Without providing both, spiritual transformation is unlikely.

Here's a simple way to do this: Challenge students, especially near the end of a series, to take immediate action. Have them write letters to God, participate in an appropriate service project, or do secret acts of love. Perhaps the best way to make sure this happens is to ask this question before beginning any series: *What's the one truth I believe God wants to plant in the hearts of students?* Then teach deeply on that truth throughout the series and end the series by connecting that truth to an action. This will help move the *hearing* and *obeying* principle from theory to practice.

53. AVOIDING SATURDAY NIGHTMARES

I know this has never happened to you, but bear with me as I share what was once a common experience of mine.

It's autumn—my favorite time of the year. Cooler weather. Colors changing. Football season. What more could one ask for?

It's also Saturday evening. I've enjoyed some yard work (honestly) and either watched Georgia Tech spank some lousy opponent or tossed the football with my kids. My family has just finished grilling on the deck. Our kids are bathed and tucked in bed, so Kathy and I are settling down to watch a DVD.

Then, without warning, something punches me in the gut. Blood drains from my face as my lungs gasp for air. I reach for a paper bag to combat hyperventilation. I've just been attacked by the Saturday nightmare...I just remembered I'm teaching youth group tomorrow!

This has probably never happened to you; but in case you're a slacker like me, you know the only thing to do is finish watching the movie (feeling guilty the whole time), then stay up late flipping through some "magic curriculum" for ideas on what to teach. The next day you teach a 30-minute lesson even though you never cracked the Bible in preparation. Personally, this is not the approach I want to take when presenting God's truth.

If you've ever experienced the Saturday nightmare and want to avoid it like the plague, here's a better way to prepare for communicating God's truth.

First, on Monday morning (seven days before teaching), do the lesson yourself. Notice I said "do." Don't "study" or "prepare;" treat the curriculum like a devotional study designed for you. In fact, feel free to do the lesson during your personal time with God. Don't try to figure out what students need to hear, simply allow space for God to do his work in you. Later, when teaching, what you say will be more powerful because God has worked in your life first.

Next, during the week, process what God's teaching you through this lesson. If you journaled or jotted down notes in the margin of the curriculum, read through your notes a few times. If a certain passage caught your attention, read it again.

Also, think about what God might want you to communicate to students. Were there certain parts of the lesson that really connected with you? If so, how can you best transfer these truths to teenagers? Any illustrations come to mind? You'll be shocked at how many ideas God fosters throughout the week once you've

FYI

An entire chapter is dedicated to this process in the book The Inside Out Youth Worker. *For more information visit www.insideoutyouthworker.com.*

personally engaged in a lesson (plus, it's easier than straining the creative corners of your brain at 11:30 Saturday evening). Be sure to jot down any thoughts or illustrations on your PDA or a notepad throughout the week.

Finally, find a time to put everything together, maybe Friday or Saturday morning. If you've been chewing on this stuff all week, the lesson should come together pretty quickly.

Try this approach the next time you teach. If you do, not only will you present God's truth more effectively, but also you'll be able to enjoy a Saturday night flick with your spouse.

54. MIX IT UP

The only bad teaching method is the one you use over and over again. Most of us have a favorite style of teaching (e.g., lecture, storytelling, role playing, Q&A, discussion questions, breaking into small groups, etc.). No matter how successful you are at using a specific style, if you overuse it, it'll eventually become ineffective. You need to mix it up.

To take this idea even a step further, regularly surprise students. Go offsite to teach, invite guest speakers, have panel discussions, or videotape part of the lesson from a different location. Variety spices things up and, if done right, will engage students in the discovery process.

55. TMI

The one fatal teaching flaw most common to all youth workers is trying to cover *Too Much Information.* In teaching, less is usually more. Therefore, it's far better if students walk away with a solid understanding of one biblical truth and how to live out that truth in real life than it is for them to walk away with tons of disconnected, disjointed data. The goal of teaching is to cultivate an environment that allows God's truth and grace to transform students, not to simply download information.

56. SCRIPTURE...IN THEIR OWN WORDS

My favorite TV show of all time, for scads of reasons, is *Seinfeld*. Funny. Philosophical—even though it's a show about nothing. Incredible character development. And although the morals of the characters are debased, the consequences of immorality are unmistakably shown.

My favorite feature of *Seinfeld* is that they give names to everyday stuff never before named. "Double-dipping." "The vault." "Puffy shirts." "Close talkers." "High talkers." "Low talkers." "Re-gifters." "Sidlers." The writers masterfully *paraphrased* life.

In many ways, the task of youth workers is similar to that of sitcom writers—except that youth workers are called to *paraphrase* Bible truth for everyday teenage living. In doing so, most youth workers steer clear of Bible translations filled with "thee," "thou," and "verily." However, even the most progressive translations lag when it comes to staying current with teenage phraseology. Therefore, if you really want students to encounter biblical truth, try letting *them* paraphrase Scripture. For example:

- At the start of a teaching series, gather students into groups of three or four and let them paraphrase the passage of Scripture you'll be using for the series. Then, during the next few weeks, use their paraphrases as teaching tools.
- In your small groups, pick a New Testament book to study. Each night before diving into discussion, have students paraphrase the section you're studying. Teach the lesson and afterward let students make any adjustments they think are necessary to their paraphrases. By the end of the year, your students will have paraphrased an entire book of the Bible. Talk about owning God's truth!

Perhaps the greatest feature of having teenagers paraphrase Scripture is that it enables youth workers to see if their youth are "getting" it. If they are, applaud their insights. If not, you now know what to focus on.

57. USE YOUTH CULTURE TO CONNECT TRUTH TO YOUR STUDENTS' WORLD

Try reinforcing every truth you teach with elements from youth culture. Use movie clips, music, video games, student interviews, student surveys, MySpace and Facebook sites, YouTube videos, magazines, or whatever else you can think of to help.

The key is to make sure these tools *support* the truth you're teaching. The best way to support the truth is to use tools that *complement* the truth or *clash* with it. The first props up the truth; the second points out the consequences of ignoring the truth.

Additionally, tools should always *strengthen* your content. If you're like me, you're tempted to use tools that don't really fit simply because you like the tool. Perhaps you think a certain song will add energy to the night, or you just love a particular movie clip and are dying to show it. Always remember, your primary goal must be to communicate truth. Use the tools that help you do this best, whether they're your favorites or not.

Finally, avoid using tools as a *substitute* for content. Using cultural tools as filler weakens the message.

58. BE ARTSY AND CREATIVE

I'm the world's worst artist. Even drawing stick figures are a challenge for me. But my wife and daughters are naturally artistic, and I've discovered they grab truth more deeply when it's somehow connected to the arts. For them, practically any truth is strengthened if they can interact with it by painting, sculpting, drawing, writing, or composing.

My son, although not artistic like my daughters, is into creative expression. Give him a truth to act out or create an original movie about that truth, and he'll go deeper with it than if it's just explained to him.

In both cases, the arts are used as tools, just as with discussion questions or small group conversations—ways of moving from knowledge-based information to learner-based ownership.

59. WHAT DID JESUS DO?

Remember WWJD bracelets? Rick Lawrence asked a good question recently: "Do we know Jesus well enough to know what he would do?"

Do you think your students do?

Here's a way to make sure students know the truth about what Jesus did and didn't do: Develop a *Jesus Did/Jesus Didn't List*.

> *[The early church] testified to the truth about Christ and lived by his grace. Truth was the food they ate and the message they spoke. Grace was the air they breathed and the life they lived.*
>
> **—Randy Alcorn**
> ***The Grace and Truth Paradox***

Pick a chapter in the Gospels, have students read through it, and then ask them to list the things Jesus did under a column entitled *Jesus Did*. Next, have them list the opposite to each action in a column entitled *Jesus Didn't.* For instance, if they write, "Jesus confronted false teachers with truth" under the *Jesus Did* column, they could write, "Jesus didn't embrace pluralism" under the *Jesus Didn't* column. Obviously, the more often this activity is done, the larger the list grows and the better students know the real Jesus. Post the list on the youth room wall as a constant reminder of the real Jesus.[17]

60. USE ALL FIVE SENSES

When seeking to communicate truth and grace, ask yourself this simple question: *How can I include all the senses to strengthen what's taught?* You'll be surprised by some of the ideas that pop when you use a sense grid.

More specifically, ask:

- How can students *touch* this truth?
- How can they *taste* this truth?
- How can they *smell* this truth?
- How can they *see* this truth differently than before?
- How can they *hear* this truth in a new way?

61. TAP INTO THE OTHER 166 HOURS OF THE WEEK

Truth transforms. Therefore, challenge students to allow the truth they learn during youth group to transform their attitudes and lifestyles when they *leave* youth group. But don't just challenge them; create support tools outside your program to help them. Set up school-based accountability and prayer groups students can join. Send daily email blasts with one idea of how the truth taught this week can transform their lives. Use Web sites and blogs to encourage teenagers to interact more deeply with what you taught. Even have a live chat room open 48 hours after youth group that allows students to check in, share their stories, and ask for prayer.

62. TRUTH-AND-GRACE TRIPS

Experiential learning is a powerful tool; one Jesus used all the time. Why not follow his example and use the same kind of truth-and-grace trips he used?

Fishing Trips. Is there a better way to teach what's required to "fish" for new believers? I'm no fishing fanatic, but I've known a few people who equate fishing with heaven. Tap into these individuals and design a one-day experience around fishing. Have them teach students the basic of fishing, and then get students fishing. Be sure students participate in the entire experience—baiting hooks, casting, reeling in, taking fish off the hook, cleaning, and even cooking the fish. Then, ask questions such as:

- What did you think of fishing? What did you like? What did you dislike?
- What surprised you the most?

End the day by reading Luke 5:1-11 and asking:

- What can we learn from fishing that can help us understand how God brings people to himself?
- What can we learn from fishing that'll help our group understand our role in fishing for new Christians?
- What one thing will you do differently in your relationships with your non-churched friends because of today's experience?

Sailing Trips. Again, get someone who knows the ins and outs of sailing and take a group of students sailing. Be sure your expert doesn't do all the work; have students involved in the process. End the day with a campfire and dinner. Talk about what they learned and how sailing is similar to their walk with Christ. Then read John 3:8 and ask questions such as:

- What is the Holy Spirit's role in the life of the Christian?
- How is a Christian's response to the Holy Spirit like or unlike sailing?
- How is sailing like your walk with Christ?

> *Now I commit you to God and to the word of his grace, which can build you up and give you an inheritance among all those who are sanctified.*
>
> —Acts 20:32

- What one thing will you do differently in your relationships with Christ because of today's experience?

Other ideas you can use that are similar to the latter two include:

- *Shop Class*—Have students participate in a woodworking project and discuss how Jesus builds them (i.e., how he shapes them, what tools he uses, how he has a blueprint before he starts).
- *Gardening*—Have students participate in some sort of gardening project, then discuss how Jesus grows them (i.e., watering, fertilizing, pruning, environmental issues, seasons).
- *Pottery Class*—Teach students pottery and let them create their own works of art. Then study Isaiah 45, Isaiah 64, or Romans 9 together.

63. PROVIDE ADULT SUPPORT

Adult support is something that's talked about often, but rarely is it tied to the concept of cultivating an environment of truth and grace. Yet connecting students with adult mentors, small group leaders, and accountability partners is perhaps the best idea for championing such an environment.

In recent years, there has been a huge push for student-led ministry, which is a good thing. However, while student-led ministry is great, it cannot replace the positive influence caring adults provide. Some youth workers might dispute this reality, but the evidence lines up strongly against them. Study after study not only supports teenagers' need for significant relationships with caring adults, but also most indicate students themselves realize this need. The National Study of Youth and Religion is the most intensive study ever done of American young people and their religious faith. One of its findings was that "the lives of [religious teenagers] are, compared to less religious teens, statistically more likely...to be linked to and surrounded by adults, particularly non-parent adults who know and care about them... [This] tends to contribute to more positive, successful outcomes in youth's lives."[18] In fact, lead researcher Dr. Christian Smith of the University of North Carolina states, "Adults inescapably exercise immense influence in the lives of teens—positive and negative, passive and active. The question, therefore, is not whether adults exert influence, but what kinds of influence they exert."[19]

If you want to cultivate an environment that champions truth and grace, facilitate adult-teenager relationships. It's perhaps the most practical step you can take to help students follow through in their commitments to Christ.[20]

64. INTERTWINE DISCUSSIONS & LESSONS

This is a simple, but profound question: *Why do most youth group meetings follow the format such as the one below?*

- Hangout Time: 20 minutes
- Worship Songs: 20 minutes
- Announcements: 5 minutes
- Teaching: 30 to 45 minutes
- Discussion Questions: 15 minutes

Wouldn't it make more sense to intertwine discussion into the lesson instead of saving it all for the end?

Teenagers need time to think about, discuss, and digest what's taught. If you really want to provide an environment that allows truth to sink in, next week change the last two bullet points of the typical youth group format to look something like this:

- Teaching: 7 minutes
- Discussion: 7 minutes
- Teaching: 5 minutes
- Discussion: 10 minutes
- Teaching: 10 minutes
- Discussion: 5 minutes
- Wrap-Up: 5 minutes

> *However, I consider my life worth nothing to me; my only aim is to finish the race and complete the task the Lord Jesus has given me—the task of testifying to the good news of God's grace.*
>
> —**Acts 20:24**

65. QUESTION OF THE WEEK

Have a box somewhere in the youth room that allows students to anonymously drop in written questions. Every week, pull out a question and let students grapple with it, then help them resolve it.

To keep this from becoming a "hot topics" practice, try to come up with some questions of your own. For example:

- If God is in complete control and he loves us, why do bad things still happen?
- What are the seven deadly sins in Scripture?
- How could Jesus be completely God and completely human?
- How do you measure spirituality? By consistency in devotions or by lifestyle? Support your answer.

66. WHAT WOULD JESUS ASK?

Speaking of asking questions, here's a twist to the WWJD movement. Instead of trying to figure out what Jesus would do, why not ask students the questions Jesus asked. The Gospels are loaded with Jesus questions. Here's a sample list just from the book of Luke:

Luke 6:46: "Why do you call me, 'Lord, Lord,' and do not do what I say?"

Luke 11:11-13: "Which of you fathers, if your son asks for a fish, will give him a snake instead? Or if he asks for an egg, will give him a scorpion? If you then, though you are evil, know how to give good gifts to your children, how much more will your Father in heaven give the Holy Spirit to those who ask him!"

Luke 12:25: "Who of you by worrying can add a single hour to your life?"

Luke 18:7-8: "And will not God bring about justice for his chosen ones, who cry out to him day and night? Will he keep putting them off? I tell you, he will see that they get justice, and quickly. However, when the Son of Man comes, will he find faith on the earth?"

Luke 22:48: "Judas, are you betraying the Son of Man with a kiss?"

67. RECREATE JESUS' PARABLES

Jesus told simple stories, called parables, which encased deeper spiritual realities. This became one of his primary teaching tools, and it only makes sense that we focus on Jesus' parables and make them one of our primary teaching tools as well. Let's face it: If it was good enough for Jesus...

How can we do this? Consider teaching a parable at least once a month or do a couple of series a year on Jesus' parables. No matter what your approach, be sure to help students connect the story to the deeper spiritual truth. Ask questions such as:

- How does this parable describe God or Jesus?
- How does this parable describe the Christian life?
- What's the simple message of this parable?

You can take this idea a step further and have students recreate parables. I've had students role play parables numerous times, and each time the parable's truth seems to stick just a little bit better. I've also been part of activities that allowed students to use paint, crayons, and sculpting clay to retell a parable. Again, the hands-on activity created sticking points for truth.

Jason Ostrander, a youth ministry friend of mine, went even a step further and had a couple of teenagers shoot a short film based on the Parable of the Good Samaritan. The film was shown one morning during the teaching time at a conference. More than 600 students were riveted to the screen. At the end of the film were instructions for how teenagers were to spend the next 30 minutes. There was no worship band or speaker, just a movie...and it was one of the most powerful teaching moments I've ever experienced.

68. WRITE YOUR OWN PARABLES

Since a parable, at its core, is a truth wrapped up in a story, youth workers can write their own parables to communicate biblical truth. Here are a few steps to consider:

Step 1: It's usually best to start by zeroing in on the truth you want to teach rather than on a story you want to tell.

Step 2: Once you have the truth, narrow it down to the one thing you want the students to grasp. In fact, get it down to one objective statement. For example, "I want students to know that God's unconditional love is a free gift."

Step 3: Find cultural illustrations of how you can communicate your objective statement. For instance, if you live near the beach, think of ways you could use surfing, waves, water, or sand. Or think about common factors in the world of students such as school, dating, gaming, movies, and hanging out with friends.

Step 4: Write a simple story that communicates the truth. The important word here is *simple.*

Here's an example of how this can be done. Joshua Becker, of Essex Alliance Church, wanted to communicate God's love to students, so he told them this story.

Imagine you're a young man about to get engaged. You find yourself in the most unique position: You have to choose between two young ladies who you're confident would both accept your proposal. You're faced with a difficult, important choice.

To make the decision even more difficult, the two young ladies happen to be identical twins, identical in almost every way. They look exactly the same. They have the same degree of intelligence. They have the same hobbies, interests, and goals. They both like to cook, do the dishes, change diapers, mow the lawn, shovel the snow, and change the oil (as long as we are being hypothetical, we might as well sweeten the deal). On the surface, there's nothing that separates one from the other. However, there is one piece of helpful information you've discovered about the women: You know that Twin A loves you with an incredible love, and Twin B hates you with the same amount of passion.

Twin A loves you and wants nothing more than to give you the best life possible. Her love for you is unconditional, abundant, and extravagant—even to the point that she would give up everything, even her own life, to bring you joy and peace.

Twin B, on the other hand, hates you. She wants nothing more than to make your life miserable. And she's going to do whatever it takes to ultimately contribute to your death and destruction.

Now who gets your wedding ring? Obviously, you're going to choose to ask Twin A to marry you. The decision becomes an easy one with that additional info.

The Word of God and the reality of life make it clear that all humans have only two options with their lives: We can choose to follow God, or we can choose to follow the world and our sinful desires. We can choose to follow a God who loves us with an unconditional love, or we can choose to chase after the world that offers temporal joy, but eternal destruction. The decision may appear to be difficult at times as the world tries to lure us, but it's only hiding its true intent. The more we comprehend how much God loves us, the more apt we are to choose to follow God because we know that the one who loves us will lead us into real, lasting joy.[21]

69. *LECTIO DIVINA* AND THE IGNATIAN METHOD

Lectio Divina, or divine reading, is an ancient spiritual practice that incorporates Scripture reading and prayer into one holistic event. It involves *reading, reflecting, responding,* and *resting*. The Internet is loaded with Web sites that can help you design a *Lectio Divina* experience for your group, but the following is the basic flow of the practice:

Read a passage of Scripture and reread the passage slowly and gently until a word or phrase draws your attention.

Reflect on what God may be saying to you. Ask: What are you saying to me today, God? What am I to hear in this passage?

Respond by expressing your deepest thoughts, feelings, and desires in dialogue with God. Your prayer may express a wide range of emotions or ideas.

Rest in God's gracious, loving presence.

The Ignatian Method is named after Ignatius of Loyola (1491-1556). This method of connecting with God encourages individuals to encounter Scripture as a sort of virtual experience by attempting to recreate the story in their minds by using all the senses God has given us. This is not a "new age" experience based solely on your imagination; it's a spiritual practice that encourages the use of your God-given imagination to think deeply about the truths of Scripture.[22]

Truth is the most valuable thing we have.

—**Mark Twain**

70. THE SCORRE METHOD

Haddon Robinson, the Harold John Ockenga Distinguished Professor of Preaching and President at Gordon-Conwell Theological Seminary, writes, "A sermon should be a bullet and not buckshot. Ideally each sermon is the explanation, interpretation, or application of a single dominant idea supported by other ideas, all drawn from one passage or several passages of Scripture."[23]

I like this "bullet" word-picture. What's more, I think it should be the goal of every talk or lesson a youth worker prepares. Having a clear, well stated objective focuses our communication.

I've read numerous books on communication, and most have a suggested method for how to create focus. The best book I've read is *Secrets of Dynamic Communication* by Ken Davis. It's simple, straightforward, and has helped me tremendously in the area of communicating truth. Ken teaches a concept called the SCORRE Method, and here's what he says about it:

> The two primary functions of the SCORRE process are the following:
>
> 1. It will serve as a *scope* to help you focus on a single objective, just as the scope on a gun blocks out all but the very center of the target.
> 2. It will provide you with a logical framework so you can construct a bullet of truth that will not miss.
>
> Here is a brief overview of how SCORRE accomplishes those goals. SCORRE is an acronym. The S stands for subject, the C for central theme, the O for objective, the R for rationale, the second R for resources, and the E for evaluation.
>
> S = Subject
> C = Central Theme
> O = Objective
> R = Rationale
> R = Resources
> E = Evaluation[24]

Anyone who doesn't take truth seriously in small matters cannot be trusted in large ones either.

—Albert Einstein

To find out more about this process, check out Ken's book.

71. "PUT IT INTO REALITY" BIBLE STUDIES

This idea comes from a good friend of mine, Dave Irwin. He's the middle school pastor at Christ Community Church in Omaha, Nebraska. When he told me how he combines the elements of community and truth in his small groups, I was blown away. It's powerful. Here's Dave's idea:

> The impact an adult leader has in the life of a student is in direct proportion to the amount of time that leader spends with the student; especially time spent outside the church setting. And therein lies the problem. Most volunteers don't have the time to spend with students outside of a church setting in addition to their work, family, and ministry commitments. And to be honest, most students don't have the time for it, either! So here's what we did to help give our leaders more time with students... *We restructured our small groups and made each lesson two weeks long!*
>
> The first week looks very similar to what we've been doing for years. We provide lessons for our leaders to facilitate with the group. These lessons explore a topic such as serving and include Scripture to read, blanks to fill in, and questions to discuss.
>
> The next week looks very different. It covers the same topic as the previous week, but from a "put-it-into-reality" perspective. The first week students *hear* that Jesus was a servant, and that he wants us to serve. During the second week students go out and *do* it.
>
> In the example of serving, we provided leaders with a list of 10 names and phone numbers of contact people in various agencies around the city (I'd spoken with these organizations in advance so they knew our leaders were going to call). Once the groups decided who they wanted to serve, the leader called the contact person and set up the details. Then students went and "did" the Bible study.
>
> Restructuring our groups this way means we've cut how much information we cover during the year, but what we gain is well worth the tradeoff. In fact, we saw an immediate difference! Students walk away from the "experience nights" with lasting memories far stronger than any group lesson gives them. Take Brian, for example. He's now a freshman, but he still talks about the time his group went around and asked for food donations to send to Katrina victims. He vividly remembers one woman who

broke down in tears when they asked if they could pray about anything for her. Wow!

What makes this approach even more powerful is how it combines teaching and relationship building. Not only are students living out the principles they learn, they also spend significantly more time with their leaders. What's more, the time spent together is packed with a higher degree of potentially life-changing experiences. Coaches hang out with their students, share a life experience with them, and coach them spiritually, all in one shot. Going back to Brian's story, his leader, Dan, felt like a hero that day for being a part of that experience with his group. He was overjoyed as he shared the story with me, and how much he had connected with his guys. You don't get moments like this over a milkshake at the mall.

Making this change has cost us a few things and pushed us to be more creative, but it's also shown everyone that we value both relationships and teaching enough to carve out time in our ministry structure to make both happen.

As a side note, this idea would work very well in the house group structure mentioned earlier.

NOTE: The next three ideas are a look at the essential principles for making structural decisions regarding the communication of truth and grace to teenagers. These ideas aren't programs to implement, but instead are ideas that should push you to consider whether you're effectively structuring your truth-and-grace environment.[25]

Keep in mind the following three essential elements to consider when making structural decisions:

- The need for *regularity*.
- The need for a *methodical* approach.
- The importance of *parents*[26]

72. THE NEED FOR REGULARITY

The National Study of Youth and Religion (NSYR) discovered "a significant supply-side dynamic operative in the religious and spiritual lives of U.S. teenagers. It appears that the greater the supply of religiously grounded relationships, activities, programs, opportunities, and challenges available to teenagers, other things being equal, the more likely teenagers will be religiously engaged and invested."[27] Additionally, not only does the statistical data from the NSYR overwhelmingly support this statement, it also demonstrates that teenagers who are regularly involved in religious activities generally do significantly better in practically every important life outcome: "Risk behaviors, quality of family and adult relationships, moral reasoning and behavior, community participation, media consumption, sexual activity, and emotional well-being.[28]

> *Being a Christian is more than just an instantaneous conversion; it is like a daily process whereby you grow to be more and more like Christ.*
>
> **—Billy Graham**

This all points to the fact that regular attendance in religious activities is extremely important in regard to life outcomes. In high-risk behavior areas such as smoking, drinking, drugs, sexual activity, media consumption, and poor grades, students identified as "devoted" statistically scored better than any other group, and in most cases dramatically so. The same is true for such positive factors as emotional well-being, relationships with adults, relationships with parents and family members, moral reasoning, and community involvement.[29] "Highly religious teenagers appear to be doing much better in life than less religious teenagers...We also believe that the empirical evidence suggests that religious faith and practice themselves exert significant, positive, direct, and indirect influences on the lives of teenagers, helping to foster healthier, more engaged adolescents who live more constructive and promising lives."[30]

Once-a-month meetings for teenagers will not impact them. In fact, even depending on once-a-week programming is likely to fall short. The idea here is simple: Look to provide two or three weekly opportunities for exposing teenagers to theological truth. Do that with regularity and you stand a better chance of impacting your students for the long term.

Practically speaking, this doesn't mean you have to program more. If you already have something on Sunday morning and/or midweek, simply supplement those times with creative interaction. Have live follow-up chats online, set up a touch-base instant message meeting, or provide an ongoing blog. The key is to meet *regularly* and follow up *regularly*.

73. THE NEED FOR A METHODICAL APPROACH

Regular programming is only one essential structural element. What actually happens during regular programs is as important, if not more important, in order to engage teenagers with truth and grace. To do this, both biblical stories and biblical theology should be methodically taught. There are a number of ways to accomplish this goal. For instance, different programs can focus on different themes. If a youth ministry offers two weekly programs, one could focus on studying different biblical stories and the other could focus more on the key theological themes found within Scripture or a practical book of the Bible.

A second method is to make sure teaching is age appropriate. For example, middle school lessons training could revolve around creeds, statements of faiths, and the gospel stories, while high school training could focus on study of books of the Bible, the entire story of God (i.e., creation through Christ), and major theological themes.

A third approach is to offer a program that provides

CHECK THIS OUT

Kenda Dean, in her book Practicing Passion, *addresses the lack of theological training for teenagers: "If we seek God's transformation for adolescents—and if we hope to convince them that Christianity is worth the trouble—the mainline church must reclaim passion, and specifically God's passion in Jesus Christ, as fundamental to our identity.... It will shift youth ministry's emphasis away from sociology, psychology, anthropology, educational theory—not to mention car washes and lock-ins—toward theology, and especially practical theology, that form of theological reflection concerned with Christian actions. This is not to say that youth ministry as practical theology never needs car washes or lock-ins, only that these youth activities—like all church activities—are harnessed for a larger purpose: To enlist young people in the mission of God." (p. 21)* electives (e.g., Bible and Theology 101, 201, 301, and 401). In this approach, 101 classes would be the most basic, and 401 classes would be the most comprehensive. Additionally, students who choose higher levels of study could be expected to be more involved with the topic by way of assignments or weekly discussion groups.

The basic principle is that a methodical approach to teaching is needed. Youth ministries that have traditionally embraced "fly-by-the-seat-of-our-pants," "hot topics," behavioral modification, sociological approaches, or psychological approaches instead of biblical and theological approaches are not giving students what they need. Their greatest need is to be regularly, and methodically, exposed to the story of God and theological truth.

74. THE IMPORTANCE OF PARENTS

Here are some surprising facts about the typical teenager:

- He places a high value on having a good relationship with parents.
- Parents greatly influence him (either positively or negatively).
- Youth ministries must invest in parents if teenagers are to become spiritually grounded.

I'd go so far as saying that if everything else is done correctly in youth ministry with regard to communicating truth and grace, yet parents don't adequately train their children theologically, the chance of students understanding and living out truth and grace is greatly diminished. As Doug Fields writes, "I've come to realize that I can have little long-lasting influence on a student's life if the parents aren't connected to the same spiritual transformation process that we're teaching at church. While students may think you're nice and feel safe talking to you, parents are the primary influencers in students' lives."[31] Christian Smith agrees: "The single most important social influence on the religious and spiritual lives of adolescents is their parents.... The best social predictor, although not guarantee, of what the religious and spiritual lives of youth will look like is what the religious and spiritual lives of their parents *do* look like."[32]

This means that youth ministries, once and for all, must realize part of their responsibility is to equip parents so they can theologically train their children. This doesn't mean you have to train parents how to parent teenagers (a difficult task if you're single, newly married, or haven't experienced parenting teenagers yourself). It *does* mean, however, that we need to teach parents how to do what we know how to do—train young people in the truth and grace of God's Word (at least, we should know how to do this). Youth ministries must get back to seeing their roles in the theological development of teenagers as *supplemental* to what parents should be doing on an ongoing basis at home.

How do we do this? By providing tools parents can use to own the responsibility of training their children. For instance, you could:

- Host seminars designed to train parents how to teach the Bible to their kids.
- Provide theological classes that parents and teenagers can take together.
- Use parent meetings to equip parents in how to cultivate environments conducive to spiritual conversation with their children.

The key is to encourage, support, train, and build parents' confidence so they'll own the responsibility of creating environments for spiritual development within their homes.

75. FROM TRUTH-AND-GRACE 101 TO 401

The depth and nature of the truth and grace you share with students will vary depending on your audience. As Paul said, "Brothers and sisters, I could not address you as spiritual but as worldly—mere infants in Christ. I gave you milk, not solid food, for you were not yet ready for it. Indeed, you are still not ready" (1 Corinthians 3:1-2). Your group might not be ready for the meatier elements of God's truth and grace, or you might have some students who are ready and eager, while others seem to care less. So what's a youth worker to do? Follow Christ's example.

For instance, if your group is just forming and is not yet ready for "solid food," you're in a similar position from which Jesus started. He first had to gather a following. Next, he had to teach them the basics about the Messiah (remember, most Jews of Jesus' day believed the Messiah would be a military or political figure), and finally, he had to reveal himself as the Messiah. This took time.

Interestingly, if one reads the Gospels without having a clear understanding of Jesus' timetable, a distorted understanding of his ministry can develop. This is what happened to me. For years I believed Jesus hit the ground running after his baptism and temptations in the wilderness. Why? Because the way the Gospels are laid out, it seems as though Jesus stuff (i.e., miracles and healings) happened instantly. But when I took a closer look at a timeline of Jesus' life, such as the one spelled out in *The NIV Harmony of the Gospels* by Robert Thomas and Stanley Gundry, I realized Jesus sort of wandered around for 18 months following his baptism and temptations. Don't get me wrong: Jesus wasn't trying to find himself; his wandering was very purposeful. As Jesus indicated near the end of this 18-month period in Mark 1:38, he traveled from village to village to share his message with as many people as possible and cultivated a movement.

> *You need milk, not solid food! Anyone who lives on milk, being still an infant, is not acquainted with the teaching about righteousness. But solid food is for the mature, who by constant use have trained themselves to distinguish good from evil.*
>
> **—Hebrews 5:12-14**

A closer look at this season of Jesus' ministry reveals some interesting facts about his truth-and-grace environment that will help us if we're starting from scratch. For instance, only two recorded miracles took place during this period—turning water into wine and the healing of the nobleman's son. What's more, both could be classified as private miracles when compared to the more public miracles such as the feeding of the 5,000 or raising Lazarus from the dead. What does this tell us about Jesus' early ministry? That he was careful about revealing too much truth too early. It's as if he wanted people to first see him without all the bells and whistles.

Additionally, truth-and-grace events such as the Sabbath controversies in John 5 and the Sermon on the Mount in Matthew 5 to 7 didn't take place until 18 months after Jesus started his public ministry. Think about it. That's basically halfway into his ministry. Though a casual reading of the Gospels makes it appear as if Jesus came out of the gates firing truth bullets from his teaching gun, that wasn't his approach at all. He started by calling people to follow him and do life with him. This kind of approach allowed him to reveal truth and grace as much by how he lived as by what he said.

So at first, Jesus was simply with his followers, showing them his heart and passions. Once they knew him, they started realizing this guy was special. That's when Jesus began backing up his claims with powerful miracles. This "more exciting" period—the second half of his public ministry—is what made it into the pages of the Gospels, which makes sense. The second half of his ministry is where all the action took place. Barely anything is written about the slower first half of his ministry. Only John writes in detail about this part of Jesus' ministry, and he devotes only the first four chapters to it.

So, if you're in the beginning stages of starting a youth group, and your students can only handle spiritual milk, follow Jesus' example. Focus on relationships and living out truth and grace. Teach them the basics of who Jesus is, what he has done for them, and who they can be in him. As they get to know Christ, they'll realize he's someone special. When that happens, you can take them deeper.

If you have a more established group, you likely have students who're ready and eager for deeper truth, while others seem to care less. If this is your situation, you can still follow Jesus' example. Notice that Jesus' followers had different levels of understanding, and the nature and depth of truth revealed to these different followers varied. For example, Jesus taught truth to the crowds. However, after the first public rejection of his teaching by Jewish leaders in Matthew 12:22-50 (again, about 18 months into Jesus' ministry), Jesus began to speak in parables as a way to teach his followers while concealing truth from his enemies. As Thomas and Gundry write, "[Parables] exhibited a new phase of the Lord's teaching. As a teaching tool, parables enabled him to continue instructing his disciples without giving his enemies unnecessary opportunities to catch him in his words (Matthew 13:13)."[33]

It's important to remember there were more than 12 followers of Jesus. After his ascension into heaven, for instance, there were at least 120 believers (Acts 1:15). This means Jesus' following, even during the toughest days, included more than 12 people. Yet the 12 were at a higher level than the rest of his followers. They made up Jesus' ministry team, so to speak. And out of those 12, three seemed to be his primary leaders (Peter, James, and John). Jesus would often slip away with the 12 for extended time of relationship building, and this time included the revelation of deeper, more meaningful truth. But he also slipped away from the 12 with just the three and did the same thing (e.g., the Transfiguration in Matthew 17).

What this means for you is if you're working with an established ministry, you'll likely have different levels of students. Some will be like the crowd, and the amount of truth revealed to them will be more milky than meaty. Others will be solidly committed to your group and can handle deeper truth. Still others, those at the ministry and leadership levels, should be challenged with even more truth. And probably most importantly, the higher the level, the more accountability should be required. Remember Jesus' conversation with Peter in John 21? Each time he asked Peter if he loved him, Jesus followed up with the challenge, "Feed my sheep." In other words, meaty teaching isn't just giving more information; it means calling for a deeper commitment.

Such an approach sounds great, but how does a youth worker determine who's ready for meatier truth? Easy...let students decide. When developing programs, target different levels of students with different programs instead of trying to make all programs be one-size-fits-all experiences. Then let students decide what programming they want to attend. Usually students gravitate to the highest level of programming for which they feel ready, which means they'll be involved in that program, as well as all the programs below that level. As an example, here's how an established ministry I led did it:

- **Outreach-level opportunities:** The focus was on the basic truth and grace of Jesus—telling students who Jesus is and what he can do for them.
- **Growth-level opportunities:** We had two types: House groups revolved around Bible study, prayer, and accountability. We also offered a deeper-level weeknight program focused on extended worship and in-depth theological training. Multiple electives were offered, and our desire was to provide interested students with a solid theological experience similar to receiving a one-year Bible and Theology certificate from a respectable Bible college.
- **Ministry-level opportunities:** The focus here was on living truth and grace. We trained students in peer-level relational ministry (e.g., Circles of Concern), and put little emphasis on the tasks of youth ministry (e.g., drama team, worship band).

BONUS IDEAS: SUGGESTED RESOURCES

Want to go deeper with cultivating an environment of truth and grace? Check out some of these great resources:

- www.echothestory.com (This is one of the best theological sites I've found. Here is how the Web site describes their mission: "Through a process called *Chronological Bible Storying* ['storying'], we help people learn how to interact with Bible stories. This method involves telling Bible stories in sequential order and leading others through a time of dialogue and discovery. Through this dialogue time, truths from each story emerge. This approach has been used in many different contexts and is proven to help people discover God's redemptive plan and realize a new connectedness of truths found in the Bible." Awesome resource.)
- *Secrets of Dynamic Communication* by Ken Davis
- *Soul Searching* by Christian Smith and Melinda Lundquist Denton (for understanding today's youth culture)
- *The Grace and Truth Paradox* by Randy Alcorn
- *Ideas Library* CD-ROM by Youth Specialties
- www.ministryandmedia.com (A great resource that empowers youth workers to tap into elements in the youth culture and use them as teaching tools; I especially like their movie clips resources.)
- *The Inside Out Youth Worker* by Kent Julian and Rick Lawrence (There's an entire chapter dedicated to helping volunteer youth workers prepare a "transformational Bible study" in two hours or less.)

PREFACE TO PART 4

The Son of Man did not come to be served, but to serve, and to give his life as a ransom for many.

- Jesus -

Serving-and-Sharing. Our working definition of *serving and sharing* has more to do with lifestyle than projects. Don't misunderstand: Service projects are a tremendous tool for cultivating an environment of serving and sharing, but they're an elementary step. The ultimate goal of an environment of serving and sharing is for students to embrace serving and sharing as a way of life. Even more, this lifestyle must also be holistic; in other words, one that seeks to serve the needs of whole people instead of exclusively caring for just spiritual needs. A serving and sharing environment especially equips and empowers students to minister to peers—both believers and nonbelievers—through a lifestyle of truth and grace. This means the focus of serving and sharing is *outward* from the body of Christ to others.

Serving and sharing were major priorities for Jesus, so much so that he challenged his followers time and time again with statements such as, "Many who are first will be last, and the last first" (Mark 10:31). These sorts of declarations never sat well with his disciples. Yet in Acts, we see the church actively serving and sharing as a way of life, and many ended up dying for the cause of grace and truth. What happened?

CLICK—JESUS BEGAN WITH THE END IN MIND

One more time, let's get a clear picture of Jesus' fulfilled vision from the book of Acts. In Acts 2:42-47 we see the early church's strong commitment to serving others. All believers "had everything in common," which means they shared with each other. They went so far with this, in fact, that they were willing to sell possessions in order to give to anyone in need. They also made it a habit to have each other in their homes and share meals together. These *expressions* of serving caused them to enjoy the favor of all people, which indicates they were respected citizens known for their generosity, hospitality, and compassion. God was adding to their numbers daily, and one of the tools God used to bring people into the movement was the environment of serving and sharing.

Other examples of serving and sharing abound in the book of Acts. Here's a sampling:

- In Acts 3:1-10, Peter and John responded to a crippled man's request for financial assistance by meeting his greater, physical need. This one act of service resulted in:
    - The man's holistic praise of God (the physical act of jumping and leaping indicates his overflowing emotions of joy and gratitude).
    - Peter sharing the message of grace and truth with onlookers (Acts 3:11-25).
    - Peter and John boldly proclaiming Christ before the Sanhedrin (Acts 4:1-22).
    - The early church praying for more opportunities to minister grace and truth (Acts 4:23-31).
- In Acts 4:32-37, once again we see that serving had become such a lifestyle choice among the early church members that they were willing to share everything. They sold property and used the proceeds to help people in need.
- In Acts 6:1-7, the apostles created a system that empowered the early church to holistically serve its diverse population. Notice that different leaders were in charge of different types of service (some were to meet the spiritual needs of members, while others were to meet the physical needs of members). What's more, the "proposal pleased the whole group" (verse 5).
- Notice that serving and sharing meant reaching outside the Jewish church to the "lost" world. It started with Philip preaching in Samaria (Acts 8:4), followed by him sharing Christ with the Ethiopian eunuch (Acts 8:26). In Acts 10, Peter traveled to Cornelius' house, which resulted in spreading the gospel to the Gentile world. And from Acts 13 on, the primary message of the book revolves around Paul's missionary journeys and the expansion of the church.

- Reading Acts and the Epistles demonstrates that the commitment to serving and sharing seen in the early Jerusalem church was passed along to the gentile churches. Paul, the primary missionary of the early church, didn't advance a "get saved" message only. His message was a "kingdom" call that revolved around the lordship of Jesus. In the outstanding book *What Saint Paul Really Said,* N.T. Wright notes: "Paul's mission should not be thought of, then, merely in terms of individualistic evangelism, rescuing souls one by one for a future heaven. To be sure, in announcing the gospel of Jesus Christ as Lord he challenged every single hearer to submit in obedient faith to the lordship of Jesus Christ."[34] Pragmatically, this meant living the serving and sharing lifestyle of Jesus, who himself said, "[I] did not come to be served, but to serve" (Matthew 20:28).
- Perhaps the two quintessential passages that capture the true nature of serving and sharing are Philippians 2 and 1 Corinthians 13. "In your relationships with one another, have the same attitude of mind Christ Jesus had" (Philippians 2:5). He came to serve, not be served. Of course, the best way to serve others, whether believers or nonbelievers, is to love them holistically.

So again, serving and sharing means holistically reaching out to others, both believers and nonbelievers, in order to share Jesus' message of grace and truth. Acts and the Epistles clearly demonstrate that the early church embraced this environmental vision of Jesus. So much so that in Colossians 1 (approximately 28 years after Jesus' death), Paul wrote: "The gospel is bearing fruit and growing throughout the whole world—just as it has been doing among you since the day you heard it and truly understood God's *grace*" (v. 6).

CULTIVATE—JESUS CREATING A TRANSFORMATIONAL ENVIRONMENT

The culture of serving and sharing seen in the book of Acts finds its start, again, in the ministry of Jesus. Remember, from the beginning Jesus knew his followers would be responsible for spreading his kingdom message. This reality influenced how he led, which means the fully developed snapshots of serving and sharing seen in the book of Acts actually had their origins in the Gospels. Jesus lived, taught, and modeled serving and sharing to those within his movement. Later, his disciples cultivated this same environment within the DNA of the early church.

TRAINING FOR SERVICE AND SHARING

Notice how the serving and sharing we see in the book of Acts has simple beginnings in the ministry of Jesus. Two specific elements stand out. First, Jesus *trained* his most responsive followers how to serve and share. He didn't teach them everything all at once; instead he used a step-by-step process in which one step built upon the previous one, and each step was more focused and intentional. For instance, here's how Mark documents Jesus' training method:

- In Mark 1:16-20 Jesus challenged Simon and Andrew to fish for men. This challenge came at least a year after he initially started calling people, including Simon and Andrew, to follow him.
- In Mark 3:7, just before the Sermon on the Mount (18 months into his public ministry), Jesus attempted to withdraw with his disciples. Pulling back with his ministry team became a common theme during the second half of Jesus' ministry. Up to this point, Jesus' focus seemed to be more on traveling from village to village in order to develop a movement. From this point on, however, it appears Jesus was less concerned about whether the

REMINDER

As stated elsewhere, a casual reading of the Gospels can cause one to miss the "timeline" of Jesus' ministry. What this means is that readers who are unaware that the Gospels focus significantly more on the second half of Jesus' public ministry than the first might be led to believe that Jesus appointed the 12 early in ministry and started equipping them immediately. However, a careful examination of Jesus' ministry timeline reveals that he called people to follow him early on, yet he did not appoint the 12 from among those followers until approximately halfway through his ministry. Therefore, his training initiatives intensified and became more focused during the second half of his ministry, likely because up to that point, he hadn't decided who was going to lead the church. Once that decision was made, Jesus became much more intentional about equipping those individuals.

movement was growing and more concerned about establishing the future leadership of the movement. It's as if he now knew his key players and was more intentional about pulling away from the crowds with these players (other examples include Mark 6:31-33 and Mark 7:17).

- Jesus not only pulled away with his key players, he also challenged them with the deeper kingdom concepts (Mark 7:18). He even went so far as to attempt to keep his whereabouts hidden (Mark 7:24 and Mark 9:30) so he could intentionally teach his disciples more deeply and prepare them to lead his movement.
- In Mark 9, even though Jesus was committed to equipping the 12, he pulled out Peter, James, and John for a higher level of revelation and equipping. He did this at least three other times (Mark 5:37; 13:3; 14:33).

EXPERIENCING SERVING AND SHARING

A second feature that stands out regarding the way Jesus equipped his most responsive followers is that he gave them opportunities to *experience* serving and sharing. In other words, his equipping wasn't only content-based; it had practical handles. Again, he used a step-by-step process in which each step built upon the previous ones, and each step was more focused and intentional. Dann Spader has attempted to map out the five major training "tours" of Jesus from his study of the harmony of the Gospels:

> **Ministry Experience #1: The Samaria Tour** (John 4:4-42—approximately one and a half years into ministry). Early in his ministry, Jesus invited his disciples to

CHECK IT OUT

"When it is all boiled down, those of us who are seeking to train men must be prepared to have them follow us, even as we follow Christ (1 Corinthians 11:1). We are the exhibit (Philippians 3:17f; 1 Thessalonians 2:7-8; 2 Timothy 1:13). They will do those things which they hear and see in us (Philippians 4:9). Given time, it is possible through this kind of leadership to impart our way of living to those who are constantly with us."

—Robert Coleman
The Master Plan of Evangelism

"come and see" *through Samaria*. This is approximately a four to six-day journey. Jesus involved his disciples in simple ways, such as getting the food (verse 8), and challenged them to "open your eyes and look at the fields! They are ripe for harvest" (v. 35).

Ministry Experience #2: The Galilee Tour (Mark 1:35-39—approximately two years into ministry). Having challenged his ministry team to become fishers of men, Jesus now shocked them by turning his back on the crowds and going throughout Galilee. During this time he cleansed the leper (Mark 1:40-45), forgave the paralytic (Mark 2:1-12), and called Matthew to join him (Mark 2:13-17). Obviously, this tour stretched the disciples' understanding of the kingdom Jesus was proclaiming.

Ministry Experience #3: Multiple Towns (Luke 8:1-3—approximately two and a half years into ministry). On this occasion, Jesus took his disciples and several women followers with him as he proclaimed the good news of the kingdom of God. These disciples, especially the women, were so eager to be with him that they supported him out of their own means.

Ministry Experience #4: Sending Out the 12 (Matthew 9:35-11:1—approximately three years into ministry). Jesus went on another tour through towns and villages, teaching in the synagogues. The size of the crowds during this tour was tremendous, and Jesus had compassion on them and challenged his disciples to "Ask the Lord of the harvest, therefore, to send out workers into his harvest field" (Matthew 9:38).

Ministry Experience #5: Sending Out the 72 (Luke 10:1-24—approximately three and a half years into ministry). Jesus sent out a second generation of workers, the 72. When they returned, the 72 reported, "Even the demons submit to us in your name" (verse 17). Jesus was "full of joy through the Holy Spirit" (verse 21). This is the only time Jesus is described as being full of joy. Why? He gave numerous reasons, one being that his disciples were blessed to see what prophets and kings of long ago wanted to see—the kingdom of God being established on earth. Amazingly, not only were these followers seeing it, but they were also part of the team doing it.[35]

YOUR TURN!

Just as Christ's vision of serving and sharing was fleshed out through the training and experiences he provided his followers, so, too, will your vision of serving and sharing be fleshed out through the training and experiences you provide your students. Remember, it was this dual approach over an extended period of time that cultivated an environment of serving and sharing among his team. Over time these environmental pieces gelled together so true serving and sharing started happening.

More specifically, Jesus' example teaches us that we must be intentional and focused when it comes to engaging students in serving and sharing. We need to follow the same sort of step-by-step approach Jesus used, first challenging students to see the harvest field, and then equipping them to go into the harvest field and get their hands dirty.

Whenever possible, share Christ; if necessary, use words.

- St. Francis of Assisi

76. MODEL SERVING-AND-SHARING

Perhaps the greatest way for teenagers to learn how to serve and share with others is for them to see you do it. Next time you visit a church member in the hospital or serve a neighbor, invite students to go with you. And be sure to be intentional. Use the opportunity to talk about why you serve others, how you look for ways to share Christ's love, the rewards that come with serving and sharing, and even your frustrations.

> *We do not attract what we want, but what we are.*
>
> **—James Lane Allen**

77. PARENTS' NIGHT OUT

Here's a simple idea that gives students a taste of serving. Once a month, or once a quarter, host a Parents' Night Out for members of your church by arranging to have students provide babysitting at the church for three or four hours. Provide the service free of charge, and if parents insist on donating money, designate the donation to go to something other than your youth ministry (a local charity or children's organization would be great). Remember, the idea is to serve with no strings attached.

78. HOLIDAY CAROLING

Another great way to initiate students into the art of serving and sharing is to take them caroling at a nursing home. But here's a twist: Don't just go caroling at Christmas, go caroling on every holiday! Even if you just picked the major holidays, your group would carol for Thanksgiving, Christmas, Easter, and Independence Day. If you go to the same nursing home, your students would actually start building relationships with many of the residents.

79. ADOPT A GRANDPARENT

Take the caroling idea above and add this idea as a way to help students move from a service *project* mentality to serving others as a *lifestyle* mentality. Here's how it works.

After one of your caroling events, introduce the idea of adopting some of the residents at the nursing home to your students. Say something such as, "Why don't we adopt our new friends as grandparents?" Be sure to explain what would be required:

- Regular visits (at least monthly)
- Cards and presents on special occasions, such as birthdays and holidays
- Regular notes and/or phone calls (again, at least monthly)

Also consider having house groups and/or small groups adopt grandparents.

Many students will discover this experience both rewarding and empowering. They'll feel good about serving someone, yet they'll also grow in wisdom and maturity as their "grandparent" speaks into their lives. That's what happens when serving moves from a project to a lifestyle. True friendships develop.

80. SECRET ACTS OF KINDNESS

Sometimes getting teenagers to serve peers feels like scaling Mt. Everest—one step forward, three steps back.

For instance, let's say one evening you hit a home run in regard to challenging students to serve each other. In fact, they all respond with, "Sign me up! I'm ready!" Yet somewhere between "Amen" and the all-out sprint for pizza, the serving idea gets shelved as a hand-to-hand combat match breaks out between two hungry deep-dish lovers. Can you say, "One step forward, three steps back"?

> *We serve God by serving others. The world defines greatness in terms of power, possessions, prestige, and position. If you can demand service from others, you've arrived. In our self-serving culture with its me-first mentality, acting like a servant is not a popular concept.*
>
> **—Rick Warren**

Since true Christianity isn't just about what people think or say, but about how they live, it's critical to help students do more than talk about serving friends—we need to get them serving. A great tool to use is Secret Acts of Kindness.

A secret act of kindness is defined as doing something positive for someone without bringing recognition to oneself. It could be sending a card, carrying someone's lunch tray, helping out with homework, slipping candy into a person's locker, or giving a different compliment to someone every day for a week. Pretty simple, huh?

Well...not so fast. As with all ideas, talk is cheap. Actually seeing teenagers move from idea to action can be a daunting task. Therefore, consider using some of the following ideas when encouraging students to do secret acts of kindness for each other:

Email reminders. It's easy for students to forget an assignment made during a weeknight meeting, so send encouraging emails to students every day to jog their memories.

The lab approach. Turn your next retreat into a Secret Acts of Kindness lab. Write each student's name on separate 3x5 cards. Pass out cards on the first day and encourage students to perform a secret act of kindness that day for whomever's name is on their card. Pass out new cards each day. By the end of the weekend, most students will have performed at least three kind acts.

Do it as a group. Pick a person in your church to serve. Have your group come up with a dozen acts of kindness they could do for this person. Choose two and plan how to carry them out secretly. The greatest fun in this experience is seeing:

a. Which students can actually keep a secret.
b. The "victim" trying to figure out who is being so nice and why.

As an FYI, if you have house groups and/or small groups, this is a great exercise to try.

81. PUT YOUR MONEY WHERE YOUR MOUTH IS

Teach tithing and giving in such a way that students see these principles more as opportunities to serve than obligations. Constantly remind them of how blessed we are, and that God expects us to bless others through what God's blessed us with. Challenge students to give money, above and beyond their church offering, to missionaries or charitable organizations or to support a child through groups such as Compassion International.

82. RENT A TEENAGER

Here's a Rent a Teenager fundraiser with a twist. Instead of using this gimmick as a way to raise money for the youth ministry budget, use it as a way to raise money for missions, for a Compassion International child, or for some other worthy cause. It'll have a triple-whammy effect: 1) Students will serve (free of charge); 2) Students will raise money for a worthy charity; and 3) more than likely, adults will give a little extra because of where the proceeds are going.

83. TUTORING

Why not set up an after school program for your community that includes tutoring? This idea is especially good for high school students and works especially well in urban areas. What's more, it meets a real need and gives real kids chances to experience real success.

According to Ginger Sinsabaugh, who splits her time between advertising and urban youth ministry with *SLAM! (Sunshine Gospel Ministries in Chicago)*, pushing educational goals in an urban setting is as important as pushing spiritual ones. "Lack of education is the #1 perpetuator of the poverty cycle....Starting a tutoring program or homework club is a no-brainer way to make urban kids big-brainers."[36]

This is one of those ideas that will move serving and sharing from a "project" mentality to a "lifestyle." For more information on how to start a tutoring program, check out "How to Begin a Tutoring Ministry for Children and Youth" at: http://www.kybaptist.org/kbc/welcome.nsf/files/begintcy/$file/begintcy.pdf

84. A BOTTLE OF COLD WATER IN MY NAME

This idea is easy and fun. On a hot summer day, load up the church van with coolers filled with ice and bottled water. Then head off to places where there are lots of thirsty people and offer them free drinks of water in Jesus' name. Go to the beach, a construction site, or a street corner. To make the project even more meaningful, tape a message on each bottle that says something such as: "No strings attached…from your friends at ____________________ Church."

85. MONTHLY MINIS

Want to see students learning to serve all year round? Try some of these Monthly Mini service projects.

The most eloquent prayer is the prayer through hands that heal and bless. The highest form of worship is the worship of unselfish Christian service. The greatest form of praise is the sound of consecrated feet seeking out the lost and helpless.

—Billy Graham

January: Shovel snow for those in your church who can't do it themselves.

February: Give out special Valentine's treats, cards, and flowers at a nursing home.

March: Clean a city park.

April: Host an Easter-themed puppet show at a community center or children's hospital.

May: Organize a free car wash for the community.

June: Volunteer to help during your church's VBS or Backyard Bible Clubs.

July: Wash the windows at the church or a local community center.

August: Package back-to-school supplies for needy families.

September: Rake leaves for those in your church who can't do it themselves.

October: Collect winter coats for homeless shelters to give out.

November: Serve Thanksgiving dinner to the needy (most communities have some sort of Thanksgiving dinner).

December: Organize a Toys for Tots drive.

86. PROJECT SERVE

Plan a week during the summer where the emphasis is on serving and sharing. Every day spend some time in the morning studying how Jesus calls his followers to serve others; then in the afternoon, live out what you studied. You might even want to invite students to live at the church all week to give it a camp or lock-in feel.

87. XTREME PROJECT SERVE

Take the Project Serve idea to the next level by inviting other churches in the community to join you. Can you imagine the impact of dozens of youth ministries in your town joining together to serve the community all at once? You could even line up newspaper and local TV coverage, not to brag about your youth group, but to brag about your God.

An Xtreme Project Serve would likely need to be a shorter experience… perhaps a weekend event or even just a day. But by expanding the number of churches involved, the same amount of impact could be made in your city in a shorter amount of time.

88. CONTINUE (AT HOME) WHAT PAUL STARTED

Want to see students get excited about serving and sharing in the *movement* of Christianity? Then involve them in a church plant.

Every few years, students I work with have had an opportunity to help launch a church plant during a major youth ministry conference. During one particular conference, our teenagers helped a new church with a core group of 35 to 40 people. This church met in the middle of an entertainment complex called Wonderland, which had a putt-putt course, go-kart tracks, and a killer arcade. All week our group, along with dozens of other groups, passed out flyers inviting people to a free family day at Wonderland. On Saturday, we assisted the church in hosting the family day and more than 1,000 people showed up. Talk about energy! Within a matter of months, this new church was averaging 250 people, many who were hearing about Jesus for the first time. Students still talk about that experience.

Helping a church plant doesn't have to be a one-week adventure. Your group could adopt a local church plant in your community. Students could serve by:

- Teaching children's classes.
- Setting up the church's meeting space or cleaning up after services are over (most church plants rent meeting spaces and have to set up and tear down weekly).
- Inviting youth from the church plant to your group's weekly or monthly events.
- Helping prepare mass mailings.
- Doing fundraisers and giving all the money to the church plant.

89. CONTINUE (OVERSEAS) WHAT PAUL STARTED

Many overseas churches are looking for help from American churches in establishing youth ministries. Can you imagine what such a project would do for your youth group? Within a few years, you could see God reproduce what he's doing in your group in a foreign church. What's even more amazing is that the new youth ministry will likely have the same "reproducing" genes in its DNA as your group, which means they'll likely plant a youth ministry in another church as well. Talk about a movement!

One word of advice: If you plan to plant a youth group overseas, you **must** read *Serving with Eyes Wide Open* by David Livermore; it's the best resource I know of that addresses the importance of cultural intelligence and intentionality. Even more, this book will open your eyes to all the great things an overseas church can "plant" in your ministry.

90. FRESHMAN FRIENDSHIPS

The freshman year of high school is perhaps the most transitional twelve months in the teenagers' lives. Think about it: They change schools, change position (from "running" middle school to being the "runts" of high school), and even change youth groups (if you separate middle school and high school groups). With all the changes, many students get lost in the shuffle. Your juniors and seniors can help make the transition a bit easier by "adopting" a freshman.

This was done in one of the ministries I led, and the results were nothing less than amazing. We kicked everything off with a welcome picnic in June to help us get to know the new freshman. We told them about the high school group and then explained the "Freshman Friendship" program to them. Then, during the rest of the summer, our Freshman Friendship program went into full throttle. Upperclassman emailed freshman, invited them to special events, and even hung out with them after youth group. By the time school started, most freshmen in our group were already assimilated and had plenty of church friends. This cultivated a deep loyalty to our group and made the rest of their transitions go a bit more smoothly.

91. YOU WATCH ME...

This idea is more philosophical than specific, yet it is still very, very practical. If you want to help students learn to serve and share, take them through this process:

- You watch me.
- I watch you.
- We do it together.
- You do it alone.

No matter what you are promoting, this process is guaranteed to empower students to serve and share on their own.

92. MINISTRY TRIPS

Jesus took his followers on ministry trips, and over time, these trips became more meaningful and significant. He started by going from town to town serving people, and his disciples simply followed him and watched Jesus do his thing. However, as time passed, they joined him in serving and sharing by doing little tasks (e.g., passing out bread and fish during the feeding of the 5,000, as well as by picking up the scraps). By the end of Jesus' earthly ministry, his followers had grown to the point that he could send them out two by two.

Youth workers would be wise to take a similar approach to ministry trips. For instance, start out with Training Trips in which students are equipped to serve others and given opportunities to practice on each other. Next, have them participate in a Work Camp experience in which they serve a community. From there, set up a Mission Trip and be sure to include serving and sharing opportunities during this experience. You can also take them on an evangelism experience, such as a Dare2Share conference, where they'll experience evangelism training and have the opportunity to reach out to others. The final challenge should be to help them live a serving-and-sharing lifestyle in their everyday lives.

Philip went down to a city in Samaria and proclaimed the Messiah there.

—Acts 8:5

93. SHOW ME THE MONEY!

During a mission trip or service project, give each student $10, $20, or $25 with these simple instructions: "Use this money to serve the community today." That's it. Nothing more, nothing less.

I've seen this done several times near the end of a week-long ministry experience, and the creative ideas students come up with are incredible. Students have bought lunch for the homeless, donated money to a worthy charity, purchased school supplies for organizations that work with children, and even pooled their resources so they could do something really big, such as buying a refrigerator for the community center where they were serving.

Want to take this idea to a higher level? Give them some money and challenge them to give extra from their own pockets. Let them know this is optional, that no one will ask them if they did, and they shouldn't tell others what they decide to do, either.

94. BACKYARD MISSION TRIPS

Speaking of ministry trips...when most youth workers hear "mission trips," they envision traveling to another state or country. But if *missions* is defined as ministering cross-culturally, then more than likely you have mission opportunities in your own backyard. Consider these ideas:

Mission to the elderly. Rake leaves or shovel snow. Help deliver food or serve meals. Although this isn't technically cross-cultural, it is cross-generational.

Mission to the sick. Again, although this isn't technically cross-cultural, it's still serving those who're often overlooked. Visit the neglected ones in a hospital...the ones no one goes to see. Visit children in the cancer or burn units. Take gifts, cards, and flowers to those who're overlooked by our society.

Mission to the homeless. The homeless community, in many ways, is a cross-cultural community. Work with a homeless shelter by serving food, presenting a program, cleaning, or serving wherever the shelter has a need.

After they had further proclaimed the word of the Lord and testified about Jesus, Peter and John returned to Jerusalem, preaching the gospel in many Samaritan villages.

—Acts 8:25

Mission to a cultural community in your area. Your community probably has churches that focus on various ethnicities. Contact them and see how your group can serve.

95. MINISTRY TASK TEAMS

A great way to cultivate an ongoing environment of serving and sharing within your ministry is to develop multiple ministry teams that give students the chance to serve. Many of these can even support your ministry, such as a:

- Drama Team
- Welcoming Team
- Tech Team
- Set-Up Team
- Stage Crew
- Worship Band
- Video Team
- Office/Administration Team
- Prayer Team

The key to these teams is that they are "task" teams, meaning they're designed to give students an opportunity to serve the group by performing a task. It's crucial for students to understand that doing a task once a week is not the same thing as living a serving-and-sharing lifestyle (a higher ministry goal). Explaining this properly requires a delicate balance of applauding their steps toward serving while challenging them to take additional steps.

96. MINISTRY LEADERSHIP TEAM

The additional step beyond serving on a task team is to become part of a serving-and-sharing team, which I like to call "The Servant Team."

What's the difference?

Most youth groups have student ministry teams such as the ones listed in Idea 95, and most are primarily task focused. In other words, each team has a specific *task* to perform in order to help the youth ministry program run smoothly.

But here's a question: Is the fulfillment of different tasks the ultimate goal in ministering to others? Or to put it another way, do these tasks represent the kind of ministry to which Jesus called his disciples? Don't misunderstand: Tasks are important and can be considered ministry. Yet the truest form of ministry is *lifestyle.* It's about relationally reaching out to others by serving them and sharing your life with them.

Think about it this way...those who're searching spiritually can act in dramas, run sound systems, or set up chairs, but true redeeming ministry can only be done by redeemed people. The point isn't that task teams are evil; the point is that we paint a poor picture of ministry if it is only connected to tasks. It gives the impression that a person can show up at church, do a task, and be done with ministry for the week. But as we know, ministry isn't just about doing tasks; it's a way of life!

So how does a youth worker expand the vision of what serving in ministry looks like? There are numerous ways to address this challenge, but one that's worked well for me is to create two levels of ministry teams. The first level, which was already explained, is task teams. In the youth groups I've led, these have been called *Ministry Teams.*

The second level is the one in which the focus is on serving and sharing as a way of life. Usually, there's only one team, and I've called this team the *Servant Team*. Some like to use the term *Leadership Team,* but I think the word *servant* helps explain the type of student who's ready for this team. This team's primary focus should be on relational ministry—investing in ministry to those within the youth group and to unchurched friends outside the youth group.

There should be high expectation and high accountability for members of this team. Students must complete applications and be interviewed in order to join. Once a part of the team, students get more time with adult leaders, not because they're liked more than other students, but because these students are expected to minister relationally to other students inside and outside the group. Ongoing training and support are provided in order to help these students live serving-and-sharing lifestyles.

97. EVANGELISM TRAINING

Evangelism training should be offered to all students interested in learning how to share Christ with their friends (this training should be required for students who are part of something such as a Servant Team). The training should be offered regularly (at least annually) and be relationally based. Dare2Share Ministries has tons of great resources. Check out their Web site: www.dare2share.org.

98. CHRIST-IN-ME STORY

Many students have learned how to write their testimonies, yet many testimony "formulas" cause their stories to sound canned and disingenuous. Instead of giving them a prepackaged formula, a better approach is to help them learn how to genuinely articulate what God's doing in their lives. Here's how you can do this:

Step One—Snapshots. Help students visualize their Christ-in-Me stories by looking at different "snapshots" from their lives. Tell them to think of their lives as a scrapbook of memory pictures. Encourage them to think through significant relationships, experiences, and events—both the comfortable ones and the difficult ones. Have them reflect on how God has been working through every detail of their lives and how God has been creating his story in them.

Step Two—Questions. Have students ask the following questions about their snapshots:

- Can I see God at work in ways I've never noticed before? If yes, how?
- What situations or events have brought about the greatest transformations in my life?
- If I could write one or two lessons from my life, what would they be (what has God taught me)?

Step Three—Timeline. Have students browse back through their "snapshots" one more time and pick the key events or experiences that transformed them most. Have them look for key learning times, painful experiences that God used, or key relationships. While most students will have dozens of significant snapshots, they need to trim their Christ-in-Me stories to three or four of the most significant ones.

Then have them create simple symbols or drawings for these snapshots and place them on a timeline. This little trick will help them remember how to communicate their Christ-in-Me stories to others, because it gives their stories frameworks that are easy to understand and mentally storable. Plus, they can draw their timelines on napkins or pieces of paper when telling someone their stories.

Two important points to remember: First, students' pictures can represent both positive and difficult experiences—just so long as the pictures represent how God has used life circumstances or people to challenge, change, and shape them. Second, since these are Christ-in-Me stories, be sure students include how they came to follow Christ as one of the symbols on their timelines.

Step Four—Practice. Have students practice with each other until they can share their stories effortlessly.[37]

99. LETTER WRITING

During a ministry-level trip, such as a missions trip or an evangelism trip, consider having students write an evangelistic letter back home to an unchurched friend. Our group has done this several times, and it's always been an intense but extremely significant experience. Here are some tips:

- Students might feel strange writing a letter. Remind them that it's like sending an email, just a bit more formal (and it's a pretty natural thing to do when traveling).
- If a student is writing a new friend he doesn't know well, instruct him to write a letter that will deepen their friendship. He can write about where he is and what he is doing. He can say, "Hey, our leaders told us to write a letter to a friend, so I'm writing you. I hope we can get together and hang out when I get home." Very simple and non-threatening.
- If a student is writing a good friend but hasn't talked too much about her relationship with Christ, she can use the letter to share part of her Christ-in-Me story. Again, she could write about where she is, and what she's doing, then explain that she's learning more about who Jesus is and why her relationship with him matters so much to her.

- If a student is writing a good friend with whom he's talked about Jesus, the letter can ask the friend to consider following Jesus. Again, he could write about where he is and what he's doing, then say something such as, "We've talked about having a relationship with Jesus. I'm curious...are you interested in following him? As you know, one reason I follow Jesus is ______________________________. When I get back, I'd love to share more. Could we talk about it?"
- Don't stop with the letter writing. Train students how to be prepared when they get home. Their friends might say, "Thanks for the letter," or they might hear, "Got your letter...that was sort of weird." Train them how to respond, and that no matter what they hear from their friends, the key is that they make sure their friends know the reason they wrote is they value their friendships highly.[38]

Then Philip began with that very passage of Scripture and told him the good news about Jesus.

—Acts 8:35

100. FROM SERVING-AND-SHARING 101 TO 401

A step-by-step approach is needed to help teenagers move from a service project mentality to a lifestyle of ministry. How can we cultivate an environment within ministry that encourages students to develop the eyes of a servant to the point that they live ministry as a lifestyle? Although such a feat might seem insurmountable, each small step adds up. For instance, consider how these simple steps would help:

Communicate the importance of serving and sharing at every level. Students today, perhaps more than ever, are looking to invest their lives in what they believe is important. So don't buy into the entertainment mentality of ministry, especially at the outreach level. All students should hear about the joy, excitement, and risk of serving and sharing. This means you can even talk about it during outreach-level experiences and challenge students to get off the bench and into the game.

Provide serving opportunities for students at every level. Don't just talk to students about serving and sharing; provide opportunities at every commitment level—outreach, growth, and ministry. Some youth workers wait until students are at a ministry level before giving them opportunities to do ministry, but this is a short-sighted approach. One of the best ways to cultivate ministry is to "salt" it. Giving students a taste of ministry before they are at the ministry level is a great way to help them get there. Even more, it's a great way to cultivate serving and sharing as an environmental element of your ministry.

Provide different ongoing teams for different levels of serving and sharing. As suggested earlier, a one-size-fits-all approach to ministry teams is probably not the best. Instead, why not provide two different types of ministry teams—task teams and a servant team? Task teams can handle the operations of a program while the servant team can focus on relational ministry.

Use the ladder approach. During regular programming, teach all students how to encourage each other and give them regular opportunities to do so. This teaches them to value people over stuff. That's step one. Giving students opportunities to serve others within the group by being members of a task team is step number two. Providing service projects or trips that give them a shot at serving people outside the group is step number three. Step four could be a mission trip, and step five could be joining the servant team. The point is that with each small step, students will experience ministry. Over time, and with the influence of the Holy Spirit, students will step their way into a ministry lifestyle.

BONUS IDEAS: SUGGESTED RESOURCES

Want to cultivate a deeper environment of serving and sharing? Check out some of these great resources:

- *Serving with Eyes Wide Open* by David A. Livermore (a must-read book on short-term missions)
- *Ideas Library CD-ROM* by Youth Specialties
- *Discover Your Shape* by Doug Fields (downloadable at www.simplyyouthministry.com)

- Sonlife Ministries (www.sonlife.com)
- Group Workcamps Foundation (www.groupworkcamps.com)
- Adventures in Mission (www.adventures.org)

CONCLUSION
THE BEST IDEA OF ALL

If you look at a plate of spaghetti, you notice that there are lots of individual noodles that all touch one another. If you attempted to follow one noodle around the plate, you would intersect a lot of other noodles, and you might even switch to another noodle seamlessly.

- Pam Farrel -

(from *Men are Like Waffles, Women are Like Spaghetti*)

Yikes! This book promises 101 ideas for creating a transformational disciple-making youth ministry? 25 + 25 + 25 + 25 = 100. One's missing!

Well, there's one last idea I think is the best of all. I call it the *spaghetti factor,* and a brief explanation of where it came from is probably necessary.

MEN ARE LIKE WAFFLES, WOMEN ARE LIKE SPAGHETTI

A number of years ago during an 18-hour drive from Atlanta to Omaha, Kathy and I read a book together entitled *Men Are Like Waffles, Women Are Like Spaghetti* by Bill and Pam Farrel. The premise of the book is that men process life in waffle "boxes," and women process life more like a plate of pasta. For instance, men divide their thinking into boxes and typically live in one box, and only one box, at a time—i.e., compartmentalizing. Women, on the other hand, noodle all of life together. Everything intersects everything else so that every thought and issue connects to every other thought and issue.

Without going into much more detail, let me say that both Kathy and I found this book insightful as well as downright hilarious. On several occasions I had to pull the minivan over because I was laughing so hard I was swerving into oncoming traffic. Since then, the book has meant a lot to our marriage, and the terms *waffle* and *spaghetti* have become staples of our combined vocabulary. When Kathy wants my undivided attention, she'll say something such as, "Kent, I need you to step out of that box and enter this one." When I'm having trouble understanding how Kathy has connected several seemingly unrelated thoughts during a conversation, I might say, "Honey, you're spaghetti-ing, and I'm not keeping up." Both terms have helped us communicate as husband and wife.

Interestingly, the term *spaghetti* has also helped me in youth ministry. Since my tendency is to live in one box at a time, ministry that should be fluid often ends up...uh, well...not fluid. In other words, if a ministry program is designed as a "serving" experience, then all I think about is how to make service happen. Ideas about adoration, community, or truth and grace will never pop into my mind. And why should they? This is a serving event, and I'm in my serving box.

Yet more often than not, Jesus allowed all four ACTS ingredients (adoration, community, truth-and-grace, and serving-and-sharing) to noodle together. He didn't think waffles; he thought spaghetti. So in youth ministry, I've learned it's wise to follow his example and become a spaghetti connoisseur.

IDEA 101: SPAGHETTI-ING INGREDIENTS

As you begin to work on your environment, one of your goals should be to noodle as many elements together as often as possible. Therefore, idea number 101 is my humble attempt to leave you with a few examples of how to do this.

Spaghetti Programs. If you noticed, I write a lot about house groups. I'm not trying to push house groups on your ministry; remember, this book isn't for promoting a particular program or structure. Instead, I write about house groups because they have been my way of allowing ACTS ingredients to noodle naturally.

Think with me for a moment about house groups. If you remember, a house group is simply three or four small groups that meet together in the same house. Part of the evening is given to house group activities where all the small groups do things together, and the other part of the evening is given to small group activities where small groups head to different sections of the house to share. Through this structure, the ministries I've led have been able to spaghetti all the elements very easily. Most nights included significant community-building time, both through the midsize house group environment and the small groups. Adoration experiences are also done through both, as well as truth-and-grace opportunities. What's more, house groups regularly do service projects together, and every spring, house groups host their outreaches (sharing opportunities). This approach has allowed the youth ministries I've led to noodle all four of the elements into one program.

Spaghetti Series. Another way I've seen the elements noodle together is through a series approach. For instance, say you have a four-part series on Christ-like love. Week one could follow a typical youth group meeting structure that provides an adoration experience and in-depth teaching time on what it means to love others in the body of Christ. During the second week, a community-building experience could be set up that allows your group to put into practice what was taught during week one. Week three could follow another typical youth group meeting structure by including an adoration experience and a second in-depth teaching, but this time the teaching could be on how to love those outside the body of Christ. Then, during the fourth week, a serving experience could give the group an opportunity to serve others outside your church.

This kind of approach not only incorporates all the elements, but it's also much more exciting, fresh, and meaningful than four weeks of "the same old thing."

Spaghetti Trips. This is perhaps the easiest of all three ideas. Next time you're planning a trip or retreat, include as many of the ACTS elements as possible. Since most retreats last at least 48 hours, figuring out a way to make every element fit shouldn't be too challenging. What's more, the variety of experiences that will come about by creating a transformational environment during a retreat will help drive home your retreat theme with students.

MY DESIRE REVISITED

If you remember, I wrote in the introduction that my hope was to offer you a better vision of making disciples in youth ministry than the one you might currently embrace. I didn't want to give you a one-size-fits-all strategy, but rather a picture of what a missional, contextual, environmental, process-oriented, practical youth ministry might look like. Hopefully I've accomplished that goal.

Thanks for being a learner with me. And thanks for loving Jesus and being passionate about youth ministry (if you weren't, you wouldn't have made it to the end of this book). What a joy it is to be in the youth ministry trenches with people such as you. May you work hard in your role as a cultivator of an ACTS environment, and may you leave the actual transformation to the only One who can pull it off.

NOTES

[1] Scot McKnight, Jesus Creed, http://www.jesuscreed.org/?cat=35.

[2] Stephen Covey, *The Seven Habits of Highly Effective People* (New York: Fireside, 1990), 99.

[3] From Quotedb.com: http://www.quotedb.com/quotes/2697.

[4] Covey, 99.

[5] Carl Wilson, *With Christ in the School of Disciple Building* (Fayetteville, GA: Worldwide Discipleship Assoc. Books, 1976), 202.

[6] Dann Spader, *Encounter: The Life and Ministry of Jesus* (Elburn, IL: Sonlife, 2004), 30.

[7] This experience was created by Troy Hatfield, Northwest Regional Director for His Passion Ministries (www.hpmnw.org).

[8] I originally wrote about this idea with a team of writers in a resource called *Core Impact* (Colorado Springs: The Christian and Missionary Alliance, 2003), 12-13.

[9] Steve Argue and Dave Livermore, *The Longest Deepest Time of the Year for Youth Ministry* (http://www.intersectcommunity.com/resources/articles/52).

[10] Ajith Fernando, *The NIV Application Commentary: Acts* (Grand Rapids: Zondervan, 1998), 622.

[11] Doug Fields, "The Power of Affection" (*Group Magazine,* November/December 2005), 36.

[12] The thoughts associated with this idea are excerpts from the book *The Inside Out Youth Worker* (Kent Julian, General Editor, Lawrenceville, GA: Life-on-Life Publisher, 2006), 133-134.

[13] Shad Helmstetter, *What to Say When You Talk to Yourself* (New York: Pocket Books, 1982), 21.

[14] Dann Spader, *Encounter: The Life and Ministry of Jesus* (Elburn, IL: Sonlife, 2004), 40.

[15] Rick Lawrence, *The Beeline* (Group Magazine, 2007), http://www.youthministry.com/article.asp?ID=1292.

[16] Ibid. (Note: Entire paragraph's content is an edited quotation from *The Beeline* article).

[17] Idea originally taken from *Group Magazine Live 2005* training event hosted by Group Publishing®.

[18] Christian Smith, *Soul Searching* (Oxford: Oxford University Press, 2005), 227.

[19] Ibid., 28.

[20] The thoughts associated with this idea are excerpts from the book *The Inside Out Youth Worker*, 196.

[21] *Youth Ministry Lemonade* (Lawrenceville, GA: Inside Out Youth Worker, 2007), 17-18.

[22] Both *Lectio Divina* and the Ignatian Method are used in an interactive resource entitled *Core Impact*. To find out more about Core Impact, visit www.alliance-youth.com.

[23] Haddon Robinson, *Biblical Preaching* (Grand Rapids: Baker, 1980), 33.

[24] Ken Davis, *Secrets of Dynamic Communication* (Grand Rapids: Zondervan, 1991), 18.

[25] Kent Julian, *Towards a Pastoral Theology for Millennials: Ministry Models for Reaching "Generation Y"* (presented to the Faculty of the Department of Bible and Theology at Grace University, Omaha, NE, January, 2006), 70.

[26] Ibid.

[27] Smith, *Soul Searching*, 261.

[28] Ibid., 281-219.

[29] Ibid., 221-234.

[30] Ibid., 263.

[31] Doug Fields, *Your First Two Years in Youth Ministry* (Grand Rapids: Zondervan, 2002), 105.

[32] Smith, *Soul Searching*, 261.

[33] Robert L. Thomas and Stanley N. Gundry, *The NIV Harmony of the Gospels* (New York: HarperCollins, 1988), 85.

[34] N.T. Wright, *What Saint Paul Really Said* (Grand Rapids: Eerdmans, 1997), 149.

[35] Information on the Five Ministry Tours paraphrased from the following resource: Spader, *Encounter: The Life and Ministry of Jesus*, 50-51.

[36] Ginger Sinsabaugh, *The Do's and Don'ts of Urban Youth Ministry* (Group Magazine, http://www.youthministry.com/article.asp?ID=334, 2007).

[37] I originally wrote about this idea with a team of writers in a resource called *Core Impact* (Colorado Springs: The Christian and Missionary Alliance, 2003), 27-31.

[38] I wrote about this idea with a team of writers in a resource called *Connexion* (Lancaster, PA: Life Impact Ministries, 2005), 54-56. I first saw this idea used during an OGN Conference hosted by Alliance Youth in partnership with Sonlife Ministries.